Nifty Little Paperback Joke Book for Grownups

Vol. 1

Bill Dietrich

Contents

Raffle	1
Forest Fire	1
Efficiency	2
Age	2
Who the Man	2
Three Pee	3
Heaven Worthy	3
A Bad Day	4
Nude Gambling	4
Cheap Date	4
Pig	5
Get a Job	5
Farting	5
Happy Birthday	6
Garden of Eden	6
Nun Tale	7
Pirate Tale	7
The Verdict Please	8
Beer Time	8
Beer for Two	8
Bar Talk	9
Cheap Beer	9
Arthritis	10
Drunk Driver	10
Push	11
New Room	11
10 Year Old Scotch	12
A Joke	12
Drinks On Me	12
Magic Elevator	13
Fun on the Farm	13
The Expedition	14
Job Interview	14
Alligator Shoes	15
Raising Chickens	15

Home Early	16
Shopping Trip	16
One Day at the Salon	17
Paint Job	17
Say It Slowly	18
Brain For Sale	18
Another Dummy	18
Road Trip	19
Breast Stroke	19
Sell That Car	19
Wallpaper	20
Blonde Got Robbed	20
Knitting Blonde	20
Blonde Kidnapper	21
Blonde Driver	21
In the Circle	22
Blondes in Heaven	22
Detective Work	23
Ouch	23
Going to California	24
Blonde Convention	24
Head and Shoulders	25
Therapy	25
Divorce	26
Raffle	26
Puzzle	27
Flight Time	27
Buggy Experiment	27
Babies Galore	28
Let Me Out	28
Squirrel	28
Bad Dog	29
Cat Heaven	29
Cruise Ship Parrot	30
Tale of Sweaters	30
Contagious	31
Doves of Heaven	31
Genie	32
Memory Class	32
Praying	33
Swimming	33
Cough Medicine	34

Relative	34
One Day at the Bank	34
Bra Shopping	35
Old MacDonald	35
Who's Crazy	35
Bears in Bars	36
Bar Bet	37
Sex Ed	37
Lecture	37
Hillbilly Sense	38
Bar Miracles	38
The Earring	39
It's Me	39
Baby Baby	40
Heaven Anyone	40
Alligator Trick	40
Sneeze Queen	41
Scary Landing	41
Professions	42
Tummy	42
Talent	42
Curious	43
Out Late	43
Yard Show	43
Dentist Visit	44
Problems	44
Sperm Count	45
Three Men	45
Hot Dog	45
FBI Job	46
Dead Parrot	47
Lucky Number	47
Hear's to Family	48
80 Year Old Mom	48
Shoplifter	48
What a Life	49
Just a Bite	49
Grilling	49
Birthday Surprise	50
Wedding Vows	50
Adam & Eve	51
Don't Gimme That	52

v

Therapy	52
Heaven On Wheels	52
Grandpa Tries Viagra	53
Appetite	54
Condoms	54
Goin to Vegas	55
The Birds and the Bees	55
Little Love	55
Fight Nice	56
Anniversary Lament	56
In the Dark	57
Timmy's Story	57
Weather Report	58
Beer Sale	58
Sinful Picnic	58
Raffle Ticket	59
Exercise	59
50th Anniversary	60
Rodeo	60
Golf Weather	60
Flowers	61
Hypothetically	61
Bless Me Father	61
Holy Typo	62
Poison	62
Cannibal Cookin	63
Who's the Guy	63
Honeymoon	63
Math Lesson	64
Be Strong	64
On the Hill	65
Honeymoon	65
Cigarettes	66
Last Request	66
Three Days	66
Toreador Special	67
Oh Nuts	68
Camel	68
Parrots	68
Monkey Fun	69
Robby Rooster	70
Vampire Bat	71

Wittle Wabbit	71
Gorilla Love	71
Lion Taming	72
Paw	73
Plane Game	73
Keep the Motor Runnin	74
Survival	74
Nosey Mom	75
Cupid at Law	75
Lois	76
Out of Oil	76
Quickie	76
Hey Mom	77
Young Marriage	77
Don't Cry	78
Definitely Correct	78
Farm Tale	78
Fun in the Men's Room	79
Sex Therapy	79
Dreams	79
Trade	80
Star Tiff	80
Memories	81
Handout	81
Don't We Look Pretty	82
Who's Cheating	82
Sibling Prom	83
Bang	83
Playing Doctor	84
Dopey Meets The Pope	84
Disgrace	85
Fishy Story	86
Zoomin Granny	86
Shirt Tale	87
One Night on a Train	87
Blonde Shorts	88
Chauvinist Shorts	93
Miscellaneous Shorts	94

Raffle

City boy Jimmy had just moved to the country and bought a donkey from a farmer for $100. The farmer agreed to deliver it the next day. The next morning however, the farmer drove up in his truck and said, "I'm sorry, but I have some bad news. The donkey died on the way over here."

"Well, just gimme back my money," Jimmy said.

"I can't do that," replied the farmer. "I already spent it."

"Just unload the donkey here, then," replied Jimmy.

"What are you gonna do with him?" asked the farmer.

"I'm gonna raffle him off," he replied.

"You can't raffle off a dead donkey!" the farmer exclaimed.

"Sure I can," Jimmy replied. "I won't tell anyone he's dead."

A few weeks later, the farmer ran into Jimmy and asked, "So, whatever happened with that dead donkey?"

"I raffled him off just like I said I would. I sold 1000 tickets for a dollar each! That's $900 profit," Jimmy boasted.

"Didn't anyone complain?" the farmer asked.

"Just the guy who won. . so I gave him his dollar back," he replied proudly.

Forest Fire

A photographer for a national magazine was assigned to take pictures of a raging forest fire. He was advised that a small plane would be waiting for him at a nearby airstrip to fly him over the fire. When he arrived at the airstrip, he found a small Cessna all fired up and waiting. He jumped in with his gear and yelled to the pilot, "Let's go!" As the plane took off, the photographer assessed the area and began planning his shots.

"Fly over the north side of the fire first," he told the pilot.

"Why?" the pilot asked nervously.

"I'll get great shots from that angle!" the photographer yelled.

"You mean you're not the flight instructor?" the pilot asked.

Efficiency

An efficiency expert had just ended a lecture and added a note of caution: "Be careful when trying these techniques at home."

"Why?" asked someone in the audience.

"Well, I watched my wife's dinner routine for years," the expert explained. "She made way too many trips between the refrigerator, table and stove, usually only carrying a single item at a time. One day I finally said, 'Why don't you stop being so stupid? Try carrying several things at once!'"

"Did it save time?" the person in the audience asked.

"Well," the expert began, "it used to take her 45 minutes to make dinner. Now it takes me 30."

Age

My girlfriend had just purchased a line of expensive cosmetics and was sitting in front of the mirror applying various stuff to herself when she asked me, "Honey, honestly, how old do I look?" I looked her over then replied, "Well, your skin, eighteen; your hair, twenty; your body, nineteen. ."

"Oh, you big ass kisser!" she gushed.

"Hang on," I said. "I didn't add them up yet."

Who the Man

A very mild mannered man had just finished reading a book titled "Be The Man of Your House" and was all pumped. When he got home from work, he marched right up to his wife and announced, "From now on, I am the man of this house! I am the boss and my word is law! Tonight, you will make me a gourmet meal, after which, you will rub my back while I watch whatever I want on TV. Then, you will pleasure me in bed however I say, and after that, you will give me a bath, towel dry me, fetch me my robe and put me to sleep with a back rub. And in the morning, guess who's going to dress me and comb my hair?"

"The funeral director," she said.

Three Pee

A lawyer, an economist, and a teacher were going to the bathroom. The lawyer finished, washed his hands, and used almost the entire roll of paper towels to dry his hands. "I was taught to be thorough," he said.

When the economist finished, he washed his hands, used only one paper towel, and said, "I was taught to be efficient."

The teacher finished, walked away without washing his hands, and said, "I was taught not to piss on my hands."

Heaven Worthy

A man arrived at the gates of Heaven and was greeted by Saint Peter. "I browsed your history and I didn't see any really good things that you did in your life, but I didn't see anything really bad either," he said. "If you can show me one really good thing that you did, I think I can get you in."

The man said, "Well, I was driving down the road and I saw this gang of like 30 guys assaulting a young woman. I was so mad that I stopped my car, grabbed a tire iron from my trunk and went after them. These guys were all huge and scary looking but I didn't care. This poor woman desperately needed help and all I cared about was rescuing her.

"Impressive! When did this happen?" asked Saint Peter.

"Like a minute ago," the man replied.

A Bad Day

A man was sitting at a bar just staring at his drink for over an hour, when a big wiseguy truck driver came over, took the drink and drank it. The poor man just broke down and started crying. The truck driver said, "Come on man, I was just kiddin. I'll buy you another drink. Jeeeez!"

"It's not that," the man said. "This is just the worst day of my life. First, I was late for work and my boss fired me. Then, I left to go home and found out my car was stolen. Then, I took a cab home and left my wallet with all my credit cards in the back seat. When I went in the house, I found my wife in bed with the mailman. Now, I finally get up enough courage to end my life and you show up and drink my poison."

Nude Gambling

Two casino dealers were working a craps table when a cute woman walked up and said, "I want to bet $10,000 on a single roll of the dice, but I'm usually much luckier when I'm nude."

The woman then slipped out of her clothes and rolled the dice.

"I won! I won!" she screamed, jumping up and down with delight. She then hugged and kissed each of the dealers, gathered up her money and clothes, and frolicked away.

"What did she roll, anyway?" the first dealer asked.

"I dunno," replied the other. "I thought you were watching."

Cheap Date

Worried that his son may be spending too much money on dating, Mr. Markanowicz asked him how much his last date had cost. The son replied, "About $15."

"Well," the father said, "I'm very proud of you for being smart enough to know how to have inexpensive fun."

"To be honest, Pop," the son replied, "I really wanted to do a lot more stuff, but that was all the money she had."

Pig

A man was driving down a steep, winding mountain road. A woman was driving up the same road. As they passed each other, the woman stuck her head out the window and yelled, "PIG!" The man immediately flipped her the finger and yelled back, "BITCH!" As he rounded the next corner, he crashed into a pig which was standing in the road.

Get a Job

A man walked up to the counter at the welfare office and said to the caseworker, "You know, I hate getting welfare. I'd really rather get up everyday and go to work at a job."

"You have perfect timing," the caseworker replied. "We just received a new job opening today from a very wealthy man who's in need of a chauffeur and bodyguard for his daughter. You'll spend many hours on the job so all meals will be provided. You'll also be required to escort her on overseas holiday trips, and satisfy her sexual urges if asked. The starting salary is $200,000 a year plus perks and bonuses."

"You're bullshittin me!" the man said.

"Yes, I am," the caseworker agreed. "But you started it."

Farting

A man said to his doctor, "I've got the farts, Doc. I mean, I fart everywhere. I fart in restaurants, church, the movies, wherever. My farts don't stink though, and you can't hear them either. I've only been here 5 minutes and I've already farted 7 times.

"Hmm," muttered the doctor as he picked up his prescription pad from the table and wrote out a prescription.

"Thanks, Doc. Will this stop my farting?" the man asked.

"No," the doctor replied. "The prescription is to clear up your sinuses. Next week, I want you back here for a hearing test."

Happy Birthday

John woke up on his birthday but neither his wife nor kids even said happy birthday to him. When he got to work though, his secretary, Abby, said happy birthday in a big cheery voice.

"Thank you!" he exclaimed. "That really made my day."

Nearing lunch time, Abby invited him to a nice birthday lunch, and instead of their usual Burger King, they went to a little French cafe across town. After lunch Abby said, "My apartment is just around the corner. Would you like to see it?"

"Sure, why not?" he replied.

At her apartment, John sat down on the sofa. Abby said she'd be right back and went into the bedroom. A few moments later, she returned with John's family and co-workers, all wearing party hats. John just sat there naked.

Garden of Eden

Adam was sitting in the Garden of Eden feeling lonely and asked God, "Could you create someone else to put on this planet with me? It's really lonely here."

"Well, I could make a woman for you," God answered.

"What is a woman?" Adam asked.

"A woman is a warm, generous, intelligent, loving creature who will provide wonderful companionship for you, take care of all your needs and give herself to you totally, without question or complaint," explained God.

"Oh Lord, what would such a creature cost?" Adam asked.

"The price would be one arm and one eye," God answered.
"Damn," Adam sighed. "What could I get for, say, a rib?"

Nun Tale

"I want to quit the veil," a nun said to her mother superior.
"But why, my child?" the mother superior asked.
"I want to become a prostitute," the nun replied.
"EXCUSE ME?" the shocked mother superior asked.
"I said I want to become a prostitute," the nun repeated.
"Oh thank Heavens! I thought you said *protestant*."

Pirate Tale

A pirate and a landlubber were talking in a bar. The landlubber noticed that the pirate had a real peg leg, a hook instead of a hand, and a patch over one eye.
"How did you lose your leg?" the landlubber asked.
"I lost me leg in a battle with some wretched enemies!" the pirate replied.
"How did you lose your hand?" the landlubber asked.
"I lost me hand in a bloody shark attack," the pirate replied.
"And how did you lose your eye?" the landlubber asked.
"I was sleeping on the beach one morning when a sea gull flew over me and crapped right in it," the pirate replied.
"But how could a little bit of bird crap cause you to lose your eye?" the landlubber asked.
"It was the day after I got me hook," sighed the pirate.

The Verdict Please

A man was on trial for murder and there was a lot evidence, but a corpse had never been found. During the defense's closing argument, his attorney decided to try a tricky tactic.

"Ladies and gentlemen of the jury, in the next minute or so the person presumed dead in this case will walk into this courtroom!" He then pointed towards the courtroom door and the jurors all turned and watched eagerly.

After several minutes, the lawyer said, "Ladies and gentlemen, I made up that previous statement, but you all watched the door and waited. I therefore put it to you, that there is reasonable doubt in this case as to whether anyone was actually ever killed, and as such, you must return a verdict of not guilty." The jury deliberated briefly and returned with a verdict of guilty.

"But how can this be?" the lawyer asked. "Every one of you had your doubts, and you all sat watching that door."

"Yes," the jury foreman replied, "but your client didn't."

Beer Time

One evening after a beer convention, some of the brewery presidents went out to a local bar. The president of Budweiser said to the bartender, "I'll have the king of beers, a Budweiser."

"I'll have the only beer made with Rocky Mountain spring water, a Coors," said the president of Coors.

"Give me a Coke," said the president of Guiness.

"Why are you drinking Coke?" the others asked.

"If you guys aren't drinking beer, neither am I." he replied

Beer for Two

A man walked into a bar, ordered two beers and drank them both. A few minutes later, he ordered two more and drank them both. He did this every night for a week until the bartender could no longer contain his curiosity.

"Why do you always ask for two drinks?" the bartender asked.

"I used to drink with my best friend every night," the man replied, "but he died, so I drink a second beer on his behalf."

A few nights later the man came in and ordered just one beer.

"Why only one?" the bartender asked.

"My wife made me give up drinking," the man replied.

Bar Talk

A shy guy walked into a bar and saw a beautiful woman sitting at the bar. After half an hour of building up his courage, he walked over and asked, "Could we talk for a while?"

"No, I won't sleep with you!" she yelled loudly.

With everyone in the bar now staring at them, the guy was completely embarrassed and quietly went back to his table. A few minutes later, the woman walked over to him and said, "I'm sorry if I embarrassed you. I'm a psychology student and I'm studying how people respond to embarrassing situations." The man thought for a moment then yelled as loudly as he could, "What do you mean $200!"

Cheap Beer

A man walked into a bar and asked for a beer.

"Here you go," said the bartender. "That'll be one cent."

"How much is a T-bone steak with fries?" the man asked.

"Three cents," the bartender replied.

"That's it?" the man asked in disbelief. "Three pennies?"

"Yep," the bartender replied.

"That's hard to believe," the man said. "Where's the owner?"

"Out sneaking around with my wife," the bartender replied.

Arthritis

A drunk got on a bus and sat down next to a priest. His shirt was soaked with booze, his face was covered with red lipstick marks, and he had a bottle of cheap wine sticking out of his pocket. He opened his newspaper and started reading. A few minutes later, he asked the priest, "Father, what causes arthritis?"

"It's caused by living a lazy, sinful life, being with dirty, cheap women and drinking excess alcohol," the priest replied.

"Imagine that," the drunk muttered, and he continued reading his newspaper.

The priest, now feeling bad for his harsh words, turned to the drunk and said, "I'm very sorry. I didn't mean to be so insensitive. How long have you had arthritis?"

"I don't," the drunk replied. "It says here in the newspaper that the Pope does."

Drunk Driver

A man stumbled out of a bar and made his way down the street, bumping into everything in his path. A policeman, parked across the street, watched intensely. When the man reached his vehicle, he fumbled around with his car keys, unlocked the door, got in and drove away.

The policeman took off after him, pulled him over a few blocks away and administered a breathalyzer test. The policeman was shocked when the breathalyzer test read 0. "I can't believe it!" he said. "I watched you stumble to your car and drive erratically for blocks, but the test says you don't have any alcohol in your system! How can that be?"

"Easy," the man replied. "I'm the designated decoy."

Push

A man and his wife were in bed when they heard knocking at the front door. The man looked at the clock, saw it was three in the morning and said, "I'm not getting out of bed at this hour."

The knocking continued and got louder and louder until his wife finally said, "You better go see who it is."

The man stumbled out of bed, went downstairs and opened the door to find a staggering drunk on the porch.

"Hey pal," the drunk slurred. "Can you give me a push?"

"No! It's three in the morning and I was in bed," the man shouted, as he slammed the door. He made his way back upstairs, crawled into bed and told his wife what happened.

"That wasn't very nice," she said. "Remember that night we broke down in that horrible storm and had to knock on that family's door? What would've happened if they didn't help us?"

"But this guy was drunk," he replied.

"That doesn't matter," she said. "He needs your help, and it would be wrong for you not to help him."

With a sigh, he went back downstairs and opened the door, but the drunk was gone. Figuring he couldn't have gone far, he yelled out, "Hey! Are you out there? Still need a push?"

"Yes, please," the drunk cried out from a distance.

"Ok, where are you?" the man yelled.

"Over here, on your swing," the drunk replied.

New Room

One night after having way too much to drink, a drunk decided to sleep it off at a local hotel. He took care of the paperwork at the front desk and headed up to his suite. A few minutes later, he staggered back to the desk and asked for a different room.

"But sir, you have our finest room," replied the clerk. "May I ask why you don't like your room?"

"Well, for one thing," the drunk replied, "it's on fire."

10 Year Old Scotch

A guy walked into a bar and asked the bartender for 10 year old scotch. The doubting bartender poured him 5 year old scotch instead. The man took one sip and complained, "This isn't 10 year old scotch, it's 5 year old scotch! What the hell?"

The bartender now realized that the guy really knew what he was talking about and began a friendly conversation with him.

A while later, an old man who had been sitting at the other end of the bar, stumbled over with a glass, handed it to the guy and said, "Here, taste this."

The guy took one sip, immediately spit it out and screamed furiously, "It's piss, you jackass!"

The old man nodded and said, "Yeah, but how old am I?"

A Joke

A blonde, a brunette, an Irishman, an Italian, a priest, a nun and a rabbi all walked into a bar. The bartender looked at them all for a moment then asked, "Is this some kind of a joke?"

Drinks on Me

A drunk walked into a bar and said, "Bartender, give everyone in the house a drink on me, and pour one for yourself!" The bartender did, but when he gave the drunk the bill, the drunk replied, "I haven't got it." The bartender slapped the drunk around a bit and threw him out.

The very next night, the drunk walked into the bar again and said, "Bartender, give everyone in the house a drink on me and pour yourself one!" The bartender figured the drunk couldn't possibly be stupid enough to pull the same trick again, so he gave everyone a drink, had one himself and gave the drunk the bill. Again, the drunk said, "I haven't got it." The bartender was so furious that this time he beat the hell out of him.

The very next night, the drunk walked into the bar again and said, "Bartender, give everyone in the house a drink on me."

"What, no drink for me tonight?" the bartender asked.

"Nope," said the drunk, "You get too violent when you drink."

Magic Elevator

A hillbilly family was visiting Chicago. Being their first time in a city, the father took the son to see the inside of a tall building. The son saw an elevator and asked, "What's that, Paw?"

"I ain't never seen nothin like that before," the father replied.

Just then, an extremely overweight woman walked up to it and pushed a button. The doors opened, the women entered the little room and the doors closed. The father and son watched intently as the little lights above the elevator blinked on and off.

Suddenly the doors opened again and a gorgeous twenty-four-year old woman stepped out.

"Quick, go get yer maw!" the father bellowed.

Fun on the Farm

A farmhand radioed his boss and said, "I have a little problem here. I hit a pig on the road and he's stuck in the front grate of my truck, wriggling like crazy. What should I do?"

"In the back of the truck there's a rifle," the boss replied. "Shoot it in the head and when it stops wriggling, just pull it out and throw it in one of the bushes."

"Ok," the farmhand said, and signed off.

About 10 minutes later he radioed back and said, "Boss, I did what you said. I shot the pig and threw it in a bush."

"Then what's the problem?" the Boss asked.

"The lights on his motorcycle are still flashing like crazy."

The Expedition

During a rock climbing expedition, some of the grappling hooks had given way and left the eight climbers desperately clinging to the swinging rope. Seven of the climbers were blonde and one was brunette. They all agreed that the weight on the rope was too much, and that one of them should let go before more hooks gave way. For an agonizing few moments, no one volunteered. Finally, the brunette gave a heartwarming speech and said she would sacrifice herself to save the lives of the others. The blondes all applauded.

Job Interview

A blonde was being interviewed for a job and the interviewer started with some basic questions.
"Your age, please?" he asked.
The blonde counted on her fingers then replied, "21."
"And your height?" he continued.
The blonde stood up, pulled a tape measure from her purse, measured herself then announced, "Five foot four."
Rolling his eyes, the interviewer decided to ask her a question that she wouldn't have to count or measure.
"Your name again, please?" he asked.
The blonde bobbed her head from side to side while mouthing something quietly to herself then blurted out, "Lisa!"
"What was all that about?" the confused interviewer asked.
"I was just running through that song in my head," the blonde replied, "Happy birthday to you, happy birthday to you, happy birthday dear. ."

Alligator Shoes

A blonde was visiting Florida and wanted to get a pair of genuine alligator shoes, but she was reluctant to pay the high prices that the local stores were asking. After becoming quite annoyed with the attitude of one store owner in particular, the blonde yelled, "Maybe I'll just go out and catch my own alligator!"

"Go ahead, if you you can!" the store owner replied smugly.

So, the determined blonde headed to the swamps to catch herself an alligator. A few hours later, the store owner was driving home past the swamp and spotted the blonde, standing waist deep in the water with a shotgun in her hand. As he stopped to watch, he saw a huge 8 foot alligator suddenly swimming toward her. In an instant, she shot it dead, hauled it onto the bank and set it down next to several other dead alligators. The store owner couldn't believe his eyes and just had to get a closer look. Just as he approached, the blonde flipped the alligator on it's back and whined, "Damn it, another one with no shoes!"

Raising Chickens

A blonde decided to start a chicken farm and went to the local supply center to buy a hundred chickens. A month later, she returned to the supply center for another hundred chickens, explaining to the clerk that the first batch had all died. After another month, she was back again for yet another hundred chickens. The surprised clerk asked if that batch had died too.

"Yea, but I think I know where I'm going wrong," the blonde explained. "I think I'm planting them too deep."

Home Early

A brunette, a redhead, and a blonde all worked in the same office. Every day, their female boss left work early and never returned until the next morning. Figuring the boss would never find out, the women decided to sneak off early themselves one day. The brunette was thrilled to be home early and took a nice dip in the pool. The redhead was thrilled to be able to get a facial and manicure at the beauty shop. The blonde was happy to be home early and snuck upstairs to surprise her husband. But when she peeked into the bedroom, she saw him in bed with her boss! Quietly, she went back downstairs and left.

The next day at the office, the brunette and redhead were already making their plans for another early departure.

"Not me," said the blonde. "I almost got caught yesterday!"

Shopping Trip

A blonde was shopping in a local appliance store and found a bargain she really liked.

"I'd like to buy this TV," she said to the salesman.

"I'm sorry, but we don't sell to blondes," he replied.

Really wanting the bargain, she hurried home, dyed her hair brown then went back to the store. "I'd like to buy this TV," she said to the salesman.

"I'm sorry, but we don't sell to blondes," he replied.

"Damn, he still recognizes me," she thought to herself.

She went home again, waited a few hours this time, then put on a full disguise, including new dress, makeup and sunglasses, then went back to the store.

"Excuse me, I'd like to buy this TV," she said to the salesman.

"I'm sorry, but we don't sell to blondes," he replied.

"How the hell do you know I'm a blonde?" she demanded.

"Because that's a microwave," he replied.

One Day at the Salon

A blonde went into the salon while listening to her walkman and asked the stylist for a trim. The stylist asked her to remove the headphones, but she refused, saying, "If you can't do my hair while I have my headphones on, I'll go somewhere else."

The stylist, not wanting to lose the business, agreed and started working. Suddenly, she accidentally bumped the blonde's headphones and they fell to the floor. The blonde immediately started gasping and also fell to the floor. When the stylist kneeled down to revive her, she heard a voice coming from the headphones saying, "Breath in...breath out...breath in..."

Paint Job

A blonde wanted to earn some money and was canvassing a wealthy neighborhood looking for work. At the first house she came to, she asked the owner if he had any odd jobs.

"How much would you charge to paint my porch?" the owner asked.

"How about 50 dollars?" she replied.

The owner agreed and told her that the paint and brushes were in the garage. The owner's wife had overheard the conversation and asked him, "Does she realize that the porch goes all the way around the house?"

"She should," he replied. "She was just standing on it."

A short time later, the blonde came in the house for her pay.

"You're finished already?" the man asked.

"Yes," she replied, "and I even gave it two coats!

"Great!" the man replied as he handed her the $50.

"But that's not a Porch, it's a Ferrari," she added.

Say it Slowly

Two blondes were driving through Michigan and came to a road sign that said they were almost in Ypsilanti. They argued the rest of the way about how to pronounce the name of the town until stopping for lunch. While paying for their food at the counter, one of them said to the cashier, "Can you settle an argument for us? Very slowly, please tell us where we are."
The cashier replied, "Burrrrrr - Gerrrrrrr - Kinnnnnggg."

Brains For Sale

A potential client of a hospital that was pioneering in brain transplants asked about the prices. The doctor said, "This Ph.D. brain costs $15,000. This brain, which belonged to one of the country's top scholars, costs $20,000. This blonde's brain over here costs $75,000."
"Oh my goodness!" exclaimed the client. "Why is a generic blonde's brain so much more than all the others?"
"It's never been used," replied the doctor.

Another Dummy

A ventriloquist was doing a show and going through a whole assortment of dumb blonde jokes when suddenly a blonde woman stood up and started yelling. "I'm sick of your stupid blonde jokes!" she began. "What does the color of someone's hair have to do with their intelligence? It's guys like you who keep blondes from being respected in the community and treated equally! You should be ashamed of yourself!"
The ventriloquist was now quite embarrassed and started to apologize but the blonde yelled, "You stay out of this! I'm talking to that little bastard on your knee!"

Road Trip

Two softball teams, one comprised of all blondes, the other of all brunettes, chartered a double deck bus for a week long tour. The brunette team, who had the bottom deck of the bus, was whooping it up and having a great time when one of them realized that the blondes upstairs weren't making any noise. She went upstairs to investigate and found all the blondes frozen in fear, staring at the road and desperately clutching their seats.

"What's the problem up here?" she asked the blondes. "We're all having a great time downstairs!"

"Yeah, that's easy for you people downstairs," one of the blondes replied. You have a driver!"

Breast Stroke

Three women, a brunette, a redhead and a blonde, were competing in the National Women's Breast Stroke swimming finals. The brunette came in first place and the redhead came in second. When the blonde finally finished, in last place and completely exhausted, she said to the judges, "I really hate to complain, but I'm pretty sure some of those girls used their arms."

Sell That Car

A blonde was trying to sell her car but was having a hard time because it had over 250,000 miles on it. A brunette co-worker approached her and said, "I know how you could make it a lot easier to sell, but it's not legal."

"I'll do whatever it takes." the blonde replied.

"Alright then," said the brunette. "Here's the phone number of a good friend of mine who's a mechanic. Tell him I sent you and explain your problem to him. He'll 'fix it' for you."

The following week, the women were talking and the brunette

asked the blonde if she took the car to her mechanic friend.

"Yes, and he 'fixed it' just like you said!" the blonde replied.

"Did you sell the car yet?" the brunette asked.

"No," the blonde replied. "Why should I sell it now? It only has 30,000 miles on it!"

Wallpaper

A brunette woman wanted to wallpaper her bedroom but she wasn't sure how many rolls of wallpaper to buy. She remembered that her blonde upstairs neighbor had the same size room and had recently wallpapered it, so she decided to call her.

"How many rolls of wallpaper did you buy when you did your bedroom?" she asked.

"Ten," the blonde replied.

The brunette then went and bought the ten rolls and papered the room, but she ended up with two rolls left over. Confused, she called the blonde again and said, "I bought ten rolls of wallpaper and did my bedroom, but I have two rolls left over!"

"Yea," replied the blonde. "So did I."

Blonde Got Robbed

A blonde called the police on her cellphone and reported that thieves had been in her car. "They took the stereo, the steering wheel and the entire dashboard!" she sobbed.

A few minutes later, an officer arrived on the scene and found the blonde, still sobbing and sitting in the backseat.

Knitting Blonde

A highway patrolman pulled up alongside a speeding car on the freeway. Looking through the driver's window, he was shocked to see a blonde woman behind the wheel, knitting! He immediately rolled down his window and yelled, "Pull over!"

"No!" the blonde yelled back, "Scarf!"

Blonde Kidnapper

A blonde who needed to raise some money fast, decided to kidnap a kid for ransom. She went to the local playground and grabbed the first kid she saw. The kid started to scream but she covered his mouth and dragged him into the woods.

"Shut up and you won't get hurt!" she told him. "I only kidnapped you for the ransom money." Next, she wrote a note saying, "I've kidnapped your kid. Put $20,000 in a paper bag and leave it in the trash can at the playground tomorrow morning." She then pinned the note to the kid's shirt and sent him home.

Blonde Driver

A police officer pulled over a car being driven by a young blonde woman and said, "I clocked you doing just 22, but the speed limit is 65. Why were you driving so slowly?"

"But I saw lots of signs saying 22!" the blonde replied.

"That's not the speed limit!" the officer yelled. "That's the route number of the highway!"

"I feel so dumb," she replied. "Thank you for telling me."

The officer then looked in the back seat of the car and saw that the passengers were shaking and white as ghosts.

"What's wrong with your friends back there?" he asked.

"We just got off route 140," she replied.

In the Circle

A blonde was driving her brand new sports car and cut in front of a tractor trailer, almost causing it to crash. The furious driver chased her and forced her to pull over. He then got out of the truck, drew a circle on the side of the road and told her to stand in it. Next, he pulled out a knife and cut the hell out of her leather seats. When he looked back at her though, she was smiling, so he retrieved a baseball bat from his truck and smashed her windows. He looked back at her again, only to see that she was now laughing. Now extremely mad, he took his knife and sliced her tires, but when he looked at her again, she was laughing even harder than before.

"What the hell is so funny?" he demanded.

"Every time you weren't looking, I stepped out of the circle!" she replied.

Blondes in Heaven

Two blonde women in Heaven were getting acquainted.
"How did you die?" asked the first.
"I froze to death," replied the second.
"Oh my! How does it feel to freeze to death?" asked the first.
"It's starts out very uncomfortable," said the second. "You get the shakes and pain in your fingers and toes. Eventually though, you get numb and it's not quite as bad. How did you die?"

"I had a heart attack," replied the first. "I thought my husband was cheating on me so I came home unexpectedly one day to try to catch him. I ran up to the bedroom but he was alone watching TV. Then I ran down to the basement but no one was hiding there either. Then I ran all the way up to the attic, but as I got to the last step I had a massive heart attack and died."

"What a tragedy," replied the second. "If only you had only looked in the freezer, we'd both still be alive."

Detective Work

A policeman was interviewing three blondes who wanted to become detectives. To test their observation skills, he had a picture of a suspect. He showed the picture to the first blonde for several seconds then said. "That was the suspect. How would you describe him?"

"That's easy," she said. "He only has one eye!"

"Um, that's only because it's a profile picture," replied the mildly annoyed policeman.

Next, he showed the picture to the second blonde. "That was the suspect. How would you describe him?" he asked her.

"Ooo I know!" she squealed in delight. "He only has one ear!"

"What's the matter with you two?" It's a profile picture!" he scolded. Now really aggravated, he showed the picture to the third blonde and said, "This is the suspect. How would you recognize him? And please think hard before you answer."

In an instant she replied, "He wears contact lenses."

"As a matter of fact, he does wear contact lenses!" replied the surprised policeman. "But how on earth did you know that?"

"Easy," she replied. "He couldn't wear glasses with only one eye and one ear."

Ouch

"Everything hurts today," a blonde complained to the doctor.

"What do you mean?" he asked.

"Watch," she said. First, she pressed on her leg and said, "Ouch!" Then, she poked herself in the ribs and said, "Ouch!" Then, she poked her hair and said, "Ouch! Even *that* hurts!"

"Is blonde your natural hair color?" the doctor asked.

"Yes, why?" she asked.

"I think you have a broken finger," he replied.

Going to California

A blonde was seated in the first class section of a plane. The stewardess told her she had to move to coach because she did not have a first class ticket.

"I'm smart and I have a good job," the blonde replied. "I'm staying in first class until we reach California."

The stewardess then informed the head stewardess of the situation, who again asked the blonde to move.

"I'm smart and I have a good job. I'm staying in first class until we reach California!" the blonde reiterated.

Another passenger finally whispered something in the blonde's ear and she immediately moved to the coach section.

When the impressed stewardess asked what he said, he replied, "I just told her this section of the plane wasn't going to California."

Blonde Convention

A crowd of 10,000 blondes was gathered at an arena, for a "Blondes Are Not Stupid" convention being broadcast on TV. The emcee took the stage and said, "We're here today to prove that blondes are not stupid. Can I have a volunteer?"

A young blonde made her way to the stage.

"What is 8 plus 8?" the emcee asked.

After a few seconds she answered, "11!"

"No, that is incorrect!" the emcee replied.

The 10,000 blondes in the arena chanted, "GIVE HER ANOTHER CHANCE, GIVE HER ANOTHER CHANCE!"

The emcee said, "Well, the TV cameras may have just made her nervous. Let's give her another chance. What is 6 plus 4?"

After a few seconds, she answered, "23?"

The emcee was quite disappointed, the blonde started crying and the 10,000 other blondes again chanted, "GIVE HER ANOTHER CHANCE! GIVE HER ANOTHER CHANCE!"

The emcee finally said, "Ok, one more chance! What is 2 plus 2?" The blonde closed her eyes, and after what seemed like an eternity, answered, "4?" All 10,000 blondes again began yelling, "GIVE HER ANOTHER CHANCE!"

Head and Shoulders

A blonde and a brunette were riding in an elevator when a handsome man got in. The women exchanged looks acknowledging how good looking he was. A few floors later, he got out.

"God he was good looking, but someone really should give him some Head & Shoulders," the brunette remarked.

"How do you give shoulders?" the blonde asked.

Therapy

"I'm on the road all the time and all of my clients are complaining that they can never reach me. It's really starting to make me nervous," the blonde told her psychiatrist.

"Don't you have a cell phone?" he asked.

"They're too expensive," she replied. "But I did the next best thing.

"And what is that?" he asked.

"I put a mailbox in my car," she replied.

"Um, and how's that working out?" he asked.

"Actually, I haven't gotten any letters yet," she sighed.

"Um, and why do you think that is?" he asked.

"I figure it's cuz when I'm driving around, my zip code keeps changing," she sighed.

Divorce

A judge was interviewing a blonde regarding her pending divorce and asked, "What are the grounds for your divorce?"
"About three acres, a little house and a pool," she replied.
"No," he said, "I mean what is the foundation of this case?"
"I think it's concrete and brick" she answered.
"What I mean is, how are your relations?" he asked.
"My mom is ok but my dad has a bit of arthritis." she replied.
"Do you have a grudge with your husband?" he asked.
"No," she replied, "just a driveway, but it's fine for us."
"Is there any infidelity in your marriage?" he asked.
"Yea, we have a really nice system with a CD player, radio, speaker thingies and everything," she answered.
"Ma'am, does your husband ever beat you up?" he asked.
"Not too often," she replied, "only if I forget to set my alarm."
"Lady, can you PLEASE just tell me why you want this divorce?" the flustered judge demanded.
"I don't want a divorce," she replied. "My husband does. He says he can't talk to me."

Raffle

A brunette, a redhead and a blonde each bought a raffle ticket at the office where they work. The winning numbers were announced and they each won a prize. The brunette won 1st prize, a cappuccino machine; the redhead won 2nd prize, a turbo vacuum cleaner; and the blonde won 11th prize, a toilet brush. A week later, the brunette said proudly to the other women, "I really love my cappuccino machine!"
"And I love my vacuum!" the redhead replied. "It picks up everything and it's light and easy to maneuver!"
"I didn't like that brush at all," said the blonde. "I went back to paper."

Puzzle

A group of blondes walked into a bar chanting "11 days! 11 days!" One of them was carrying a wooden picture puzzle of Cookie Monster mounted in a frame. The bartender looked at the puzzle then asked her, "Why are you chanting '11 days'?"

"Well, a lot of people think blondes are like really dumb, but we put this puzzle together in just 11 days, even though it said 1 to 2 years on the box." she proudly replied.

Flight Time

A blonde was planning a vacation and called the airport for flight information. "How long does it take to fly from New York City to Los Angeles?" she asked.

"Just a minute...," the agent began.

"Thank you!"replied the blonde. "Goodbye."

Buggy Experiment

A blonde laboratory worker was left alone with a beetle and decided to try an experiment. She pulled off one of its legs then told it to run. The beetle obeyed her command. She pulled off another leg and again told it to run. The beetle again obeyed, but with a bit of difficulty. Finally, she pulled all of the remaining legs off and told it to run, but this time it just laid there. "Oh goodie, I made a new discovery!" she squealed with delight. "A beetle with no legs goes deaf!"

Babies Galore

A blonde mom had just given birth to 6 babies and was lying in the recovery room. Her husband came in, sat by her bed, stroked her arm lovingly and asked, "How are you, my love?"
BAM! She punched him right in the face!
"What was *that* for?" he asked, rubbing his now bloody nose.
"I *told* you not to do it doggy style!" she bellowed.

Let Me Out

A young blonde was traveling for the first time and had gotten a hotel room. A day later she called her mother crying.
"Oh my God, what's wrong?" her mother asked.
"I can't get out of my room!" she wailed.
"What do you mean you can't get out? her mother demanded.
"There's only three doors!" she sobbed. "One is a bathroom, one is a closet and one has a big DO NOT DISTURB sign!"

Squirrel

A little squirrel leaped from a tree branch, did a spastic midair dance and slammed into the ground. After a few seconds, he climbed back up the tree, made his way out onto the branch, jumped and slammed into the ground again. Over the next hour, the squirrel did this over and over again. Finally, a female bird sitting nearby turned to her mate and said, "We better tell him he's adopted before he really hurts himself."

Bad Dog

A blind man was standing on a corner with his guide dog when the dog raised his leg and wet on his pants leg. The man then reached in his pocket, took out a doggie biscuit and fed it to the dog. A busybody who had been watching the whole scenario ran up and said, "You shouldn't give him that biscuit. He'll never learn anything if you reward him for bad behavior!"

"I'm not rewarding him," the blind man said. "I'm just trying to find which end is his mouth so I can kick him in the ass."

Cat Heaven

When a cat who had just died arrived in heaven, God asked her how she had liked her life on earth. She told him that it was awful. She had to sleep in cold, wet alleys, had to fight other cats for food and hardly ever had enough to eat. God told her he was sorry it had turned out that way, but that in heaven she would now be happy. He then gave her a comfortable pillow to sleep on. The cat laid down on the pillow and was happy.

A few days later, a few hundred mice came to heaven and God asked them how they had liked their lives on earth. They said that it was terrible and their feet were very sore and worn out from constantly running from cats. God felt very bad for the mice and gave them each a set of roller skates.

Weeks later, God ran into the cat again and asked her how she was enjoying heaven. She said it was great. The pillow he gave her was the most comfortable place she had ever slept, but even better than that were the yummy little meals on wheels.

Cruise Ship Parrot

A magician who worked on a cruise ship was having a problem. The captain's parrot, who frequently saw his routine, had learned how his tricks were done and had begun shouting things during his shows, like "It's up his sleeve!" or "Look, he's using a mirror!"

The magician was furious, but there was nothing he could do since it was the captain's parrot. One day, the ship sank and the magician found himself floating on a piece of plywood in the middle of the ocean, along with the parrot.

They scowled at each other for nearly two full days without saying a word, until the parrot finally said, "OK asswipe, I give up! Where's the fucking ship?"

Tale of Sweaters

Three women were sitting in the waiting room at the gynecologist's office, each of them knitting a sweater for their baby-to-be. The first one stopped knitting and took a pill.

"What was that?" The others asked.

"Vitamin C," she replied. "I want my baby to be healthy."

A few minutes later, the second woman took a pill.

"What was that?" the others asked.

"Oh, it was iron," she replied, "so my baby will be strong."

A few minutes later, the third woman took a pill.

"What was that?" they asked her.

"The morning-after-pill," she answered. "I can't get the stupid arms right on this fucking sweater."

Contagious

A third grade teacher told her class that the word of the day was 'contagious' and asked if anyone could use it in a sentence.

The first student she called on said, "You should stay away from kids with the measles cuz they're contagious."

"Good," said the teacher.

Next, she called on a little girl near the front of the room. The girl smiled and said, "Love and goodwill can be contagious."

"Excellent!" the teacher praised.

Next, she called on a troublesome little boy who never paid attention in class. "The word today is 'contagious,' now use it in a sentence." she demanded.

The boy stood up and said, "Ok. One day, me and my dad was watching the lady next door filling her pool with a pail and my dad said, 'It'll take that stupid contagious to fill it that way.'"

Doves of Heaven

Three women arrived in Heaven and Saint Peter welcomed them at the gates, saying, "You can do whatever you want here, as long as you don't step on the doves." As they looked around Heaven, they noticed that there were doves everywhere, and in a matter of minutes one of the women stepped on one. Saint Peter immediately reappeared with a hideously ugly man, shackled him to the woman and said, "For stepping on a dove, you must spend eternity chained to this ugly man."

A few days later, the second woman stepped on a dove. Again, Saint Peter appeared with an ugly man and shackled him to her.

After a few day, Saint Peter approached the third woman, this time with a very handsome man, and shackled him to her.

"What did I do to deserve this?" the thrilled woman asked.

"I don't know what you did lady, but I stepped on a dove," the man answered.

Genie

A man was walking along a California beach and spotted an old lamp in the sand. He picked it up, rubbed it and out came a genie in a cloud of smoke.

"Yea yea," sighed the genie, "you freed me from the lamp. This is like the sixth time this month. I'm sooo sick of this wishes crap! You can forget about getting three wishes. You're getting ONE. Now, hurry up and make it."

The man thought about it and finally said, "I've always wanted to go to France, but I'm afraid of flying and I get very seasick. Build me a bridge to France so I can drive there!"

"What are you, nuts?" yelled the genie. "Do the math! How would support beams ever be made long enough to reach the bottom of the ocean? I mean, all that concrete, all that steel, all those miles! No! Absolutely not! Pick something else!"

The man thought for awhile then said, "Ok, I've been married and divorced five times. I wish I had a total understanding of women. . the ability to know what they're thinking, why they're crying, why I'm getting the silent treatment, basically just to know what they really want and how to make them happy."

"You want that bridge two lanes or four?" the genie asked.

Memory Class

An elderly couple was having memory problems and took a memory class at the local senior center. A few day later, the old man was outside telling his neighbor about the class.

"What was the instructor's name?" the neighbor asked.

"Oh, uh," the old man pondered, "you know that flower, the uh, pretty one that smells nice but has those thorns?"

"You mean a rose?" the neighbor asked.

"Yea, that's it!" the old man said. He then turned toward his house and yelled, "Hey Rose, what was the instructor's name at that memory class we took?"

Praying

A father passed by his son's room one night and heard his son praying,"God bless Mommy, Daddy, and Grandma. Bye-bye Grandpa."

The next morning, they found Grandpa had died in bed of a heart attack. The father told himself that it was a coincidence.

The next night, he again heard his son praying, "God bless Mommy and Daddy. Bye-bye Grandma."

Sure enough, the next morning, they found Grandma dead on the floor. The father was scared now and decided to listen outside his son's door every night. For the next few months, his son said his prayers normally, until one night he prayed, "God bless Mommy. Bye-bye Daddy."

The father was so terrified that he stayed awake all night and went to the doctor's early the next morning for a complete physical. When he returned home, his wife was waiting on the porch. "I'm so glad you're home," she said. "It was an awful day. We found the milkman dead on the porch this morning."

Swimming

Three disabled men entered a swimming contest. The first had no legs, the second had no arms, and the third was just a head.

All three were given a push into the pool and the race was underway. The man with no legs took the lead and the man with no arms was following a close second. The head sunk right to the bottom of the pool.

Halfway through the race, the man with no legs noticed that the head had sank and swam back to save him. He made his way to the bottom of the pool, grabbed the head, brought him to the surface and set him safely on deck.

Sputtering to catch his breath, the head yelled, "I spend six years learning to swim with my ears and some jackass goes and puts a swimming cap on me!"

Cough Medicine

A pharmacy owner arrived at work and saw a man clinging desperately to one of the display counters. He ran to the back room and asked his clerk what had happened to the man.

"He wanted something for his cough," the clerk said, "but I couldn't find any cough syrup, so I gave him a bottle of laxative and told him to drink it all."

"Laxative won't help a cough, you idiot!" the owner yelled.

"Sure it will," said the clerk. "Look at him. He's afraid to cough."

Relative

A married couple had an argument in the car and had driven the last hour in silence. As they drove past a barnyard of pigs and donkeys, the wife sarcastically asked, "Relatives of yours?"

"Yep," replied the husband. "In-laws."

One Day at the Bank

A man who had been waiting in line for over 15 minutes, cut ahead of the other customers, marched up to the woman teller and said, "Lady, I've been standing in line way too long, while your incompetent ass ain't been doin shit! Now take this check and deposit it in my account so I can get the hell out of here!"

"Don't speak to me like that!" she exclaimed.

"Then do your job, genius!" he retorted.

"I do not have to take this kind of abuse," she protested as she motioned for the bank manager to come over.

"What is the problem?" the manager asked.

"I've been in line half an hour and all I wanted to do was deposit this 2 million dollar lottery check," the man explained.

"And this bitch wouldn't help you?" the manager asked.

Bra Shopping

A man walked into the ladies department of a store and said to the woman at the counter, "I'd like to buy a bra for my wife."

"What type of bra?" the clerk asked.

"Type? There is more than one type?" the man asked.

"Sure," said the clerk. "Look around. Actually though, I usually just break it down to just three types."

"And what are they?" he asked.

"The Catholic type, the Salvation Army type, and the Baptist type." she answered.

"What's the difference between those?" he asked.

"Well, the Catholics supports the masses, the Salvation Army helps lift up the fallen, and the Baptists make mountains out of molehills."

Old MacDonald

Two blondes from Sweden were taking a citizenship exam. The last question was, "Old MacDonald had a _____."
The first blonde had no idea of the answer and whispered to the other, "What's the answer to the last question?"

"You're so dumb!" the second blonde replied. "Everyone knows that! Old MacDonald had a *farm!*"

"Oh yeah, I remember now," said the first. As she started to write the answer, she paused for a moment then whispered to the first, "How do you spell farm?"

"You are really dumb, that is sooo easy! It's E I E I O."

Who's Crazy

A psychologist was making his rounds at the institution and entered a patient's room. He found patient 1 sitting on the floor playing with Legos, and Patient 2 hanging upside down from a ceiling beam by his legs.

"What are you doing?" the doctor asked patient 1.

"I'm building something," replied the patient.

"Why is your friend hanging upside down from the ceiling?" the doctor asked.

"He's crazy. He thinks he's a light bulb," the patient answered.

"If he's your friend, you really should get him down from there before he hurts himself," said the doctor.

"What? And work in the dark?" he replied.

Bears in Bars

A bear walked into a corner bar in Billings, Montana, sat down on a stool and ordered a beer.

"We don't serve beer to bears in bars in Billings," the bartender said.

"Give me a friggin beer!" the bear demanded.

"We don't serve beer to belligerent bears in bars in Billings," the bartender replied.

"Give me a beer NOW!" the bear said, banging on the bar.

"We don't serve beer to belligerent, banging bears in bars in Billings," the bartender replied.

"Now look," the bear yelled, "if you don't give me a beer right now, I'm gonna eat that lady sitting at the end of the bar."

"We don't serve beer to belligerent, banging, bully bears in bars in Billings," the bartender replied.

The bear went to the end of the bar, ate the woman, returned to his seat and again demanded a beer.

"We don't serve beer to belligerent, banging, bully bears in bars in Billings who are on drugs," the bartender replied.

"Drugs?" the bear asked angrily. "I'm not on drugs!"

"Yes you are. That was a barbitchyouate!"

Bar Bet

A man in a bar walked up to the bartender and said, "I'll bet you $500 that I can piss in this glass from across the room."

The bartender rolled his eyes, laughed and said, "Ok buddy, you got a bet."

The man then set the glass down on the bar, walked to the other side of the room, unzipped his fly and just peed all over the floor and tables. He then walked back to the bar.

"Ha ha, looks like ya missed! Pay up!" the bartender said.

With a huge smile, the man handed the bartender the $500.

"You lost $500, why are you smiling?" asked the bartender.

"I bet that guy over there $2,000 that I could piss all over your bar and all you'd do is laugh about it!" the man replied.

Sex Ed

Three teenage boys just received their grades from their sex education teacher. The first boy received a D, the second boy received a D- and the third boy received an F.

"We should get her for this," said the first boy.

"Yea!" said the second. "We should egg her car!"

"I'd like to kick her right in the nuts!" said the third.

Lecture

The dean of an exclusive women's college was lecturing the young women on sexual morality. "Young women face very difficult times today," she said. "In moments of temptation, you should ask yourself one very important question: Is an hour of sinful pleasure worth a lifetime of shame?"

A young woman in the back of the auditorium raised her hand and said, "Excuse me, how do you make it last an hour?"

Hillbilly Sense

Three hillbillies were sitting around on the porch talking.

"My wife is so dumb," the first began, "that yesterday she drug home a washin machine, but we ain't got no lectric!"

"My wife is dumber than yer's," the second argued. "She brung home a dishwasher, but we ain't got no runnin water!"

"My wife is the dumbest," the third said. "I seen a whole box of them rubbers in her purse, but she ain't got no dick."

Bar Miracles

An Irishman limped in to a bar, struggled to pull himself up onto the bar stool and asked for Irish whiskey. When he noticed Jesus sitting at the end of the bar, he said to the bartender, "Give Jesus a drink on me!"

Shortly after, a blind man with a cane felt his way up to the bar, located an empty stool, sat down and asked for a beer. After a moment, he overheard a familiar voice and said to the bartender, "I hear Jesus over there, give him a drink on me!"

A while later, a hillbilly staggered in, bellied up to the bar and asked for a shot of Jack and a beer. "Hey, ain't that Jesus?" he asked. "Give that good ole boy a drink on me!"

Later that night, Jesus walked over to the Irishman, touched his leg and said, "For your kindness, you are healed!"
The Irishman stood up, took a few pain free steps and cried out in joy, "Thank you, Lord!"

Next, Jesus touched the blind man's forehead and said, "For your kindness, you can now see!"
The blind man's vision was instantly restored and he cried out in joy, "Thank you, Lord!"

Jesus then approached the hillbilly but the hillbilly cried out in panic, "Don't touch me, Lord! I'm gettin disability!"

The Earring

A man noticed his conservative friend wearing an earring and asked, "Since when do you wear an earring?"

"It's no big deal, it's only an earring," the friend replied.

"I'm just really surprised," the man said. "So, how long have you been wearing it?"

"Ever since my wife found it in our bed," he replied.

It's Me

A group of men were sitting in the locker room at the gym. A cell phone sitting on the bench rang and one of the men pushed the phone's handsfree speakerphone button.

"Hello," he said.

"Honey, it's me. Are you at the club?" a woman's voice asked.

"Um, yea," he replied.

"I found a necklace for $2,000. Can I buy it?" she asked.

"Ok, go ahead," he replied.

The other men were quite surprised by his generosity.

"I also stopped by the Mercedes dealership and saw this year's new model. It's really nice and only $80,000!" she said.

"Ok, you can buy it." he replied.

The other men couldn't believe what they were hearing!

"And honey, that beautiful condo on Elmwood Avenue was just reduced to $320,000. Should I get it?" she asked.

"Ok, go ahead," he replied.

"Thank you honey! I love you! See you later!" she said.

"I love you too." As he shut off the phone, he glanced around the room and asked, "Anyone know who's phone this is?"

Baby Baby

A newborn baby was causing quite a commotion in the delivery room. The baby appeared to be perfectly normal, but had been laughing hysterically for his entire 3 minutes of life. He was examined by one doctor after another, but no cause for the unusual laughter could be found. Finally, one doctor noticed the baby's tightly clenched fist and gently pulled his tiny fingers open, only to find several birth control pills.

Heaven Anyone

A priest walked into a bar and said, "Anyone who wants to go to heaven, stand up." Everyone stood except for one old drunk.
"You don't want to go to heaven when you die?" the priest asked the drunk.
"When I die? Sure," the drunk muttered. "I thought you were taking a load up now."

Alligator Trick

A man with a cane and an alligator walked into a bar, but was stopped instantly by the bartender. "You can't bring an alligator in here!" he yelled.
"But he does a really cool trick," the man replied.
"Well then, show me first," the bartender said.
The man put his penis in the alligator's mouth, then hit him in the head repeatedly with his cane, but didn't get bit. The crowd that had now gathered around was completely astonished.
"Does anyone else want to try?" the man asked.
An old lady in the crowd raised her hand and said, "I do, but don't hit me with that stick."

Sneeze Queen

A man and a woman were sitting next to each other on an airplane. Suddenly the woman sneezed, then wiped her nose with a tissue and shuddered violently in her seat. A few minutes later, the woman sneezed again, wiped her nose with a tissue and shuddered violently in her seat. The man was now becoming a bit concerned. A few minutes later, the woman sneezed again, and as before, wiped her nose with a tissue and shuddered violently. The man finally turned to her and said, "Excuse me, but you've been sneezing, wiping and shuddering like that ever since we got on the plane. Are you ok?"

"I'm terribly sorry if I disturbed you," she replied. "I have a very rare medical condition that causes me to have an orgasm every time I sneeze."

"Are you taking anything for it?" he asked.

"Pepper," she replied.

Scary Landing

A plane was coming in to Dallas when severe weather caused it to stall and dive towards the ground. The pilot and co-pilot worked desperately to keep the plane from crashing, and just seconds from crashing nose first, they were able to regain enough control to land safely.

Airport officials rushed to the plane and were somewhat stunned to see 200 midgets getting off the plane. As the officials talked with the pilot, several of them commented that it was very unusual to see so many midgets on one flight.

"They weren't midgets," the pilot replied. "They were Texans with all the shit scared out of them!"

Professions

Three guys and a woman were discussing their professions. The first guy said, "I'm a YUP; Young, Urban, Professional" The second said, "I'm a DINK; Double Income, No Kids." The third said, "I'm a RUB; Rich, Urban, Biker." The woman said, "I'm a WIFE; Wash, Iron, Fuck, Etc."

Tummy

A little boy wandered into his parents room in the middle of the night and saw mommy bouncing up and down on daddy. When mommy saw him standing there, he ran back to his room.
Mommy got dressed and ran to his room to explain. "Daddy's belly has gotten bigger, and I was just flattening it for him."
"You're wasting your time, Mommy" the boy replied. "Every day when you're at work, the lady next door comes over blows it back up."

Talent

A man was sitting on a bus across from a stunning woman in a tiny miniskirt and couldn't stop staring at her thighs. When she uncrossed her legs, he realized she wasn't wearing any underwear. When the woman realized he was staring, she asked, "Are you looking at my privates?"
"Yes," the man answered sheepishly. "I'm sorry."
"It's ok," she replied. "It's talented. Watch it blow you a kiss."
Sure enough, she made it blow him a kiss.
What else can it do?" the impressed man asked.
"It can also wink," the woman replied.
The man watched in amazement as it winked at him.
"Would you like to stick a couple of fingers in it?" she asked.
"Holy crap!" he exclaimed. "It can whistle?"

Curious

A little girl walked into the bathroom unexpectedly and saw her father naked. Before he was able to cover himself, she saw that he had stuff that was different than she had.

"What were those things hanging there, daddy?" she asked.

Daddy thought for a moment and replied, "Those are God's amazing apples of life. Without those, no one would be here."

The confused little girl later mentioned it to her mother.

"Did he say anything about the dead branch they're hanging from?" her mother asked.

Out Late

Two married men were out drinking and discussing their wives. The first said "You know, I don't know what to do. Whenever I go home after I've been out late drinking, I shut off the engine and coast into the driveway. I take my shoes off and tippy toe up the stairs then quietly undress in the bathroom and carefully slide into bed, but my wife STILL wakes up and screams at me for being out so late. I hate hearing her mouth!"

"You're doing it all wrong," the other guy said. "When I get home, I screech into the driveway with the radio blasting, slam the door, march up the steps singing, jump into bed, grab my wife's butt and say 'gimme some lovin!' She never wakes up."

Yard Show

"It's too hot for clothes today," George said to his wife. "I wonder what the neighbors would think if I cut the lawn naked."

"Probably that I married you for your money," she replied.

Dentist Visit

The Johnsons entered the dentist's office and Mr. Johnson made it very clear that he was in a big hurry. "No fancy stuff," he said. "No needles, gas or any of that stuff. Just pull the tooth and get it over with."

"I wish more of my patients were as brave as you," the dentist commended. "Now, which tooth is it?"

Mr. Johnson nudged his wife and said, "Show him, honey."

Problems

The groom-to-be had a problem and went to his father. "Dad, I have a very serious problem that I fear may hurt my marriage. My feet have started smelling really bad lately. I've tried powders, creams, everything, but nothing helps," he said.

"All you have to do is wash your feet as often as you can and always wear socks, even to bed," replied his father.

The bride-to-be also had a problem and went to her mother. "Mom," she began, "when I wake up in the morning my breath is really horrible and I'm afraid he'll hate me."

"Lots of people have bad breath in the morning," her mother comforted. "It's nothing to worry about." Just get right out of bed in the morning and immediately brush your teeth."

The couple was married the next day, and by following the advice each had received, were managing quite well. After a few months, the husband woke up one morning to find that one of his socks had come off. Fearful of the consequences, he desperately searched the bed, which of course woke up his wife.

Without thinking, she asked, "What are you doing?"

"Uh oh," he said. "I think you swallowed my sock."

Sperm Count

A 70 year old man went to his doctor's office for a sperm count. The doctor handed him a jar and said, "Bring me back a sample tomorrow." The man took the jar and left.
The next day he brought the jar back empty.
"Why is it empty?" the doctor asked.
"Well doc, first I tried with my right hand, then I tried with my left hand, but no luck. Then I asked my wife for help. She tried with her right hand, then her left, but nothing. She even tried with her mouth, but still no luck. We even called the woman next door. She tried with her hands and mouth too, but no luck."
"You actually called your neighbor?" asked the doctor.
"Yep," the man replied, "but she couldn't open it either!"

Three Men

A seventy year old man said to his friends, "Every morning I wake up at 7 and have to go to the bathroom, but I have to stand there for an hour because it barely trickles out."
"That ain't so bad," replied his eighty year old friend. "Every morning at 8, I have to take a dump, but I end up sitting on the toilet for an hour because I'm constipated."
That ain't bad," said their ninety year old friend. "Every morning at 7, I piss like a racehorse, then at 8, I shit like a pig. Problem is, I don't wake up until 11."

Hot Dog!

Two foreign nuns were visiting the US for the first time and one of them remarked to the other, "You know, I've heard that these Americans actually eat dogs."
"I've heard that too," the second replied. "But if we are to live in America, then we may as well do as the Americans do."

They soon spotted a hot dog vendor and approached his cart.
"Should we try one?" the first asked.
"I believe we should," the second answered cheerily.
"Two dogs, please!" they piped to the vendor.

The vendor happily wrapped two hot dogs in foil and handed them to the nuns. Excited to try their "dogs", the nuns hurried over to a nearby bench and sat down. The first nun unwrapped hers, stared at it for a moment, then leaned over to the second nun and whispered, "What part did *you* get?"

FBI Job

Three men were at the FBI building for job interviews. The first man was called in and the interviewing agent said, "The most important requirements of an agent are loyalty and dedication." He then handed the man gun and said, "Your wife is in the next room and I want you to go in and kill her."

"I can't do that!" the shocked man replied.

"Then this job is not for you," the agent said. "Good day."

The next man was called in and the agent said, "To be in the FBI, you must be loyal and dedicated. Your wife is in the next room. I want you to go in and shoot her with this gun."

"I'm sorry," the man replied. "I can't do it."

"Then this job is not for you," the agent said. "Good day."

The last man was called in and the agent said, "To be an FBI agent, you must be loyal and dedicated. Your wife is in the next room. I want you to shoot her with this gun."

The man took the gun and went into the room. A moment later, the agent heard 6 shots, followed by a lot of smashing, banging and screaming, then silence. A moment later, the man came out of the room and said to the agent, "That gun only had blanks in it. I had to beat her with the chair instead."

Dead Parrot

A woman went to a veterinarian with her lifeless parrot. The vet listened to the parrot's chest with his stethoscope for a moment then said, "I'm very sorry, ma'am. He's dead."

"Are you sure?" the woman asked?

"Yes," answered the vet. "I'm very sure"

"How can you be so sure?" the woman demanded. "All you did was listen with that thing for two seconds. You didn't do any tests or anything. He might just be in a coma or something."

The vet sighed, left the room and returned a minute later with a Labrador retriever. The dog stood up on his hind legs, sniffed the parrot then looked up at the vet and nodded.

The vet left the room with the dog and returned with a cat. The cat immediately jumped on the table, walked around the parrot several times, then nodded at the vet and left the room.

"I'm sorry," said the vet. "But like I said, your parrot is dead."

He then went to his computer, printed out a bill and handed it to her. She looked at it and screamed, "Are you crazy? You want $500 just to tell me my parrot is dead?"

"If you had just accepted my diagnosis, it would have only been $15," he said. "But with the Lab Report and Cat Scan. . "

Lucky Number

A woman was having a really terrible day in Las Vegas and was down to her last $50. "What rotten luck!" she moaned.

A man walking by her table leaned in and said, "Try playing your age, maybe you'll get lucky," then continued on his way.

Moments later, the man heard a loud commotion and made his way back to the woman's table, where he saw her passed out on the floor with the table operator kneeling over her.

"What happened? Is she all right?" he asked.

"I don't know, buddy," the table operator replied. "She put all her money on 33, then passed out when 40 came up."

Hear's to Family

An elderly woman, who had just recently gotten a hearing aid from her doctor, was having a checkup.
"Your hearing is nearly perfect," the doctor said. "Your family must be really happy."
"Oh, I haven't told them yet," she replied. "I like listening to their conversations in the day and changing my will at night."

80 Year Old Mom

An 80 year old woman just had a baby and all of her relatives came to visit. When they asked to see the baby, the elderly mother said, "Not yet." After waiting an hour, they again asked to see the baby, but the mother again replied, "Not yet."
"When can we see the baby?" they finally demanded.
"When it cries," the mother replied.
"Why do we have to wait until it cries?" they asked.
"Because I forgot where I put it," she muttered.

Shoplifter

A woman was arrested for shoplifting at the supermarket. At her hearing the judge he asked her, "What did you steal?"
"A bag of carrots," she replied.
"And why did you steal the carrots?" he asked.
"Because I was hungry," she answered.
"And how many carrots were in the bag?" he asked.
"Eight," she replied.
"Then I will give you eight days in jail," he said.
As he was about to make the punishment official, the woman's husband stood up and asked if he could say something.
"What is it?" the judge asked.
"She also stole a can of peas," the husband quipped.

What a Life

An old man was sitting on a park bench crying his eyes out when a young man came over and asked him what was wrong.

"I'm a millionaire," he said. "I own a beautiful mansion and I'm married to a gorgeous 22 year old blonde model who pleasures me in bed however I want."

"Man, you have things any guy would love. Why the hell are you are sitting here in the park crying?" the young man asked.

"I can't remember where I live," the old man replied.

Just a Bite

An old man was walking in the city when he spotted a gorgeous woman with perfect breasts. "Hey, would you let me bite one of your breasts for $100?" he asked.

"Get away from me, creep!" she said with disgust.

"Would you let me bite it for $10,000?" he persisted.

"$10,000? Ok, one bite," she said. "But not here. We'll go in the alley."

They walked down the alley and she unbuttoned her blouse.

He immediately started caressing and kissing her breasts.

"Just bite it already!" she demanded.

"Naa, I better not," he said, "I really can't afford it."

Grilling

A husband and wife were doing some yard work. He was cleaning the BBQ grill while she was bent over weeding the garden. Glancing at her behind, the husband said, "Hey, your rear is almost as big as this grill!" She ignored the remark and continued working. That night in bed, the husband started to get frisky. The wife smugly replied, "If you think I'm firing up this grill for that one little wiener, you are sadly mistaken."

Birthday Surprise

It was a man's 29th birthday and he was picking up a package at the post office. As the clerk handed him the large, colorfully wrapped box, the man said, "That's a birthday present! It's my birthday today!"

"Well happy birthday!" the clerk said. "How old are you?"

"29," the man replied.

"Hope you have a great day!" the clerk said.

"Thank you!" replied the man. He left with his package and proceeded to the bus stop to get a bus home.

A few minutes later, an old lady walked up and sat down next to him. "Oh, what a lovely package!" she said.

"It's a present! Today's my birthday!" the man replied.

"Happy birthday!" the old lady said. "Don't tell me your age. I have my own secret way of telling how old someone is!"

"Oh yeah? How?" asked the man.

"If I can put my hand down your pants for 3 minutes, I'll tell you exactly how old you are," she replied.

"I don't believe it," he replied. "But I'm not going to let you put your hand down my pants!"

"Oh well, I guess you'll never know," she replied.

After a few minutes though, the man's curiosity got the best of him and he said, "Okay, I have to see this! Go ahead."

The old lady slid her hand down his pants and played around for 3 minutes, then stated confidently, "You are 29 years old!"

"How the hell did you do that?" he exclaimed.

"I was behind you in line at the post office," she said.

Wedding Vows

During the wedding rehearsal, the groom secretly called the priest aside and said, "I'll give you $100 if you'll change the wedding vows. When you get to the part where I promise to 'love, honor and obey' and 'be faithful forever,' leave those out." He then handed the priest a $100 bill.

Reading the vows on wedding day, the priest came to the groom's part and recited, "Do you promise to obey her every command, to bow down to her every whim, to serve her breakfast in bed every morning of your life, and swear to never even look at another woman as long as you both shall live?"

The groom gulped, looked around at all the guests then said in a tiny voice, "I do."

After the ceremony, the furious groom cornered the priest and yelled, "I thought we had a deal!"

"She made me a better offer," the priest replied, as he handed him back the $100.

Adam & Eve

One day the Lord called to Adam and said, "It is time for you and Eve to begin populating the world. I want you to kiss her."

"Yes Lord, but what is a kiss?" Adam asked.

The Lord gave him a brief description and off he went. A few minutes later Adam returned and said, "That was fun, Lord!"

"Now I'd like you to caress Eve," the Lord said.

"What is caress?" Adam asked.

The Lord gave Adam a brief description and Adam took Eve into the bushes. A few minutes later, Adam returned smiling and said, "That was even better than the kiss."

"Now I want you to make love to her," the Lord said.

"What is make love?" Adam asked.

Again the Lord gave him directions and off he went with Eve.

This time however, Adam returned in under two seconds and said, "Lord, what is a headache?"

Don't Gimme That

A man picked up a woman in a bar and took her back to his apartment, where they made love all night long. In the morning, the woman asked, "You don't herpes, do you?"

"No, I don't," the man replied.

"Thank heavens!" she said. "I never want to get that again!"

Therapy

A man said to his therapist, "Doc, I can't go on like this."

"What seems to be the problem?" the therapist asked.

"Well, I'm 40 years old and I've never had much luck with the ladies, no matter how hard I try," the man replied.

"I'm going to tell you a simple technique," the therapist said. "I want you to tell yourself every day that you are a fun person, an attractive person, and a good person. Say it often, say it with real conviction, and believe it. Be positive and outgoing, and within a week, you should have women flocking around you."

A few weeks later, the man is back at the therapist's for a checkup and looks as miserable as ever.

"Didn't my technique work for you?" the therapist asked.

"Yea, it worked great," the man replied. "The last few weeks, I've dated some very beautiful women, stayed out all night dancing, and had some of the greatest sex I've ever had."

"Then why do you look so unhappy?" the therapist asked.

"My wife is being a real nag about it," the man sighed.

Heaven On Wheels

Three men just entered Heaven and were greeted by God.

"As you may or may not know," God began, "the type of transportation you will be given here depends on how faithful you were to your spouse."

"I cheated on my wife throughout our entire marriage," the first man said. "But I am sorry now and beg forgiveness."

"I am ashamed of you," God said, "You have been a cheat all your life and I will only give you a beat up Ford Pinto."

"Please forgive me, Lord" the second man begged. "I cheated on my wife too, but it was only one time, and it wasn't totally my fault. I am sorry and I beg forgiveness."

"I am not very happy with you," God said, "but for your sincere remorse, I will give you a vehicle that will serve you well."

"I loved my wife and never cheated on her," the third man said. "I treated her like gold."

"Yes," said God, "you have proven to be a man of character, and you may choose any car you want!"

A few weeks later, the first and second man saw the third man sitting in his new, shiny red Jaguar, crying!

"What the hell are you crying about?" they asked.

"I just saw my wife on rusty roller skates," he replied.

Grandpa Tries Viagra

Grandma and Grandpa were visiting their grandson for the weekend. Grandpa was in the bathroom and happened to find a bottle of Viagra in his grandson's medicine cabinet.

"Does that Viagra work?" Grandpa asked.

"I don't use them," the grandson replied. "Uncle Joe left them here, but he likes them."

"How much do they cost," Grandpa asked.

"I think they're $10 a pill," the grandson replied.

"Let me try one," Grandpa said. "I'll slip the money under your pillow later."

The next day, the grandson found $60 under his pillow and was rather confused. "I told you they were only $10," he said to Grandpa.

"I know," Grandpa replied. "The other $50 is from Grandma."

Appetite

"Do you want some breakfast, honey?" a woman asked her husband. "I can make you some bacon and eggs, or some waffles or pancakes."

"No, thanks," he replied. "It's this Viagra. It really takes the edge off my appetite."

"How about just a cup of coffee or tea, then? Or maybe an apple, or just some toast?" she coaxed.

"No, nothing," he answered.

At lunch time she asked, "Can I make you some lunch? How about something light, maybe a sandwich or a nice fruit salad?"

"No, thanks," he replied. This Viagra really kills my appetite."

At dinner time she asked, "How about some dinner? I could make burgers, or I could run to Burger King, or I could just throw something in the microwave."

"No thanks. With this Viagra, I'm just not hungry," he replied.

"Well, will you PLEASE let me up so I can eat!" she begged.

Condoms

A man and his 8 year old son walked the condom rack in a store.

"What are these, Dad?" the boy asked.

"Those are condoms. They're for safe sex," replied the father.

As the boy inspected the large display rack, he picked up a package of 3 and asked, "Why are there 3 in this box?"

"Those are for high school boys," answered the father. "One for Friday, one for Saturday and one for Sunday."

Next, the boy he picked up a 6 pack. "And these?" he asked.

"Those are for college men," the father replied. "TWO for Friday, TWO for Saturday, and TWO for Sunday."

"And what about the 12 pack?" he asked.

"Those are for married men," the father sighed. "One for January, one for February. ."

Goin to Vegas

A man found his wife on the front porch with her bags packed.
"Where the hell are you going?" he asked.
"I'm going to Las Vegas," she replied. "I just found out that I could make $300 a night for what I give you for free!"
"Wait a minute!" the man said as he ran inside the house, only to emerge a few minutes later with his own suitcase.
"Where the hell are you going?" asked the wife.
"I'm going with you," he snapped. "I wanna see how you're gonna live on $600 a year."

The Birds and the Bees

A young girl approached her mother and asked her where babies come from. The mother thought for a moment then answered, "A mommy and daddy fall in love and get married, then go into their bedroom and kiss, hug and make love. That means the daddy puts his thingie by the mommy's thingie."
"But I looked in your room one night and you had daddy's thingie in your mouth. Why do you do that?" the girl asked.
"Jewelry, my dear, jewelry." the mother replied.

Little Love

Two dwarfs were vacationing in Atlantic City and met two gorgeous women. After a few drinks, they took the women back to their rooms. The first dwarf had impotence and had a terrible evening, but he could hear the other dwarf in the room next door grunting, "ONE, TWO, THREE, UH", all night long!
In the morning, the first dwarf said, "Last night was so embarrassing for me. I couldn't get an erection all night."
"You think *that's* embarrassing?" sighed the second dwarf. "I couldn't even get on the bed!"

Fight Nice

A husband and wife were arguing as they frequently did.

"When you die," the husband yelled, "I'm getting you a headstone that says, 'Here Lies My Wife - Cold As Ever.'"

"Oh yeah?" she retorted. "When you die, I'm getting you one that says, 'Here Lies My Husband - Stiff At Last.'"

Anniversary Lament

"Have you ever cheated on me, Sophie?" George asked.

"Oh George, why would you ask such a question now, after fifty wonderful years of marriage?" she asked.

"I'd just like to know," he replied. "Please?"

"Well, all right," she answered. "Yes, three times."

"Three? When were they?" he asked.

"Well, remember when you were 30 and you really wanted to start your business and no bank would give you the loan, but a couple weeks later, the bank president came over to the house and signed the loan papers himself?" she asked.

"Oh, Sophie! You really did that for me? I love you more than ever! When was the second time?" he asked.

"Well," she began, "Remember when you had the heart attack and needed that very dangerous operation that no one would even attempt, but then Dr Ackeldorf flew all the way out here and did the surgery himself?"

"You saved my life by doing that." he replied. "I truly couldn't have asked for a better wife. When was the third time?"

"Well," she began, "Remember a few years back when you really, really wanted to be president of your golf club but you were 14 votes short?"

In the Dark

A woman had grown tired of always having sex in the dark because of her husband's inhibitions. Hoping to cure him, she flipped on the table lamp one night while they were having sex. Much to her surprise, he was using a cucumber! "And just how long have you been using cucumbers on me?" she demanded.

"Let me explain," he begged.

"You rotten sneaky son of a bitch!" she hollered.

"Sneaky? You're calling ME sneaky?" he retorted. "Maybe you'd care to explain our two children!"

Timmy's Story

A woman just returned from a weekend business trip and her 6 year old son Timmy greeted her with, "Mommy, yesterday daddy was in the bedroom with the lady next door. Then daddy got on top of her and..."

"Shhh, don't say anymore," she told him. I want you to tell me the whole story again when your daddy gets home."

Later that day when her husband arrived home, she started yelling, "I want a divorce. I'm leaving you, you dirty rotten, cheating..."

"But why?" he interrupted. "What did I do?"

The woman immediately called their son in and said, "Go ahead, Timmy. Tell daddy the story you told me today."

"Well," Timmy began, "Daddy and the lady next door went in the bedroom and took off all their clothes and got in bed and daddy got on top of her and then they did that thing that you did with uncle Paul last year when daddy was away."

Weather Report

A husband and wife were asleep in bed at 2:00 a.m. when the telephone rang. The husband picked up the phone, but before he could say anything, some talking came from the other end. A moment later the husband yelled, "How the hell do I know! What am I, the weather man?" and slammed down the phone.

"Who was that?" his wife asked sleepily.

"I don't know," the husband answered. "Some idiot asking if the coast was clear."

Beer Sale

A husband and wife were shopping and the husband put a case of beer in the shopping cart.

"What do you think you're doing?" the wife asked.

"It's on sale, only $10 a case," he replied.

"Put it back, we can't afford it," she yelled.

A few minutes later, she put a $20 cosmetics kit it in the cart.

"Just what do you think you're doing?" the husband yelled.

"But it's makeup," she defended. "It'll make me look beautiful for you when we're making love."

"So will the beer, for half the price," he quipped.

Sinful Picnic

A middle-aged, divorced woman was starting to find life very lonely and finally agreed to go on a date with a gentleman from their church that her daughter had been trying to fix her up with.

The gentleman picked her up one Sunday and they went to a secluded place by the lake to have a picnic. Despite her initial resistance, the man finally succeeded in making love to her.

"I can't believe I let that happen," the woman remorsed. "I don't know how I'm going to face my daughter, knowing that I sinned twice with a man that I just met!"

"Twice?" the man asked. "We only did it once."

"But you *are* going to do it again, *aren't you?*" she asked.

Raffle Ticket

A woman came home from work one night wearing a brand new diamond necklace.

"Where did you get the necklace?" her husband asked.

"I won it in a raffle at work, now be a doll and make me a small bowl of cereal while I get dinner started." she replied.

The next night, she came home from work wearing long diamond strand earrings.

"Where did you get the earrings?" her husband asked.

"I won them in a raffle at work, now be a sweetie and make me a small bowl of cereal while I start dinner," she replied.

The next night she came home from work in a mink coat.

"I suppose you won that in a raffle?" the husband asked.

"As a mater of fact, I did, now be a doll and make me a small bowl of cereal while I get dinner started," she replied.

A minute later he placed her cereal bowl on the counter, but with just dry cereal in it.

"Hey, it's dry!" she whined.

"I didn't want you to get milk on your raffle ticket," he replied.

Exercise

A Lamaze class instructor announced "Exercise is especially good for you during your pregnancy! Walking is a great way to get exercise and is highly recommended. And men, it wouldn't hurt you to spend some time walking with your ladies!"

The men gazed around looking like dullards until one asked, "Is it ok if she carries a golf bag while we're walking?"

50th Anniversary

A husband and wife were celebrating their 50th anniversary and the wife was wearing the same sexy nightie she had worn on their wedding night.
"Honey, do you remember this?" she asked.
"Yes I do," he replied. "You wore that on our honeymoon."
"And do you remember what you said to me?" she asked.
"Yes, I remember," he replied.
"Well, what was it?" she asked.
"I said that I was going to suck the life out of your boobs and screw you senseless," he answered.
"Yep," she replied with a giggle. "So what do you have to say tonight?"
"Um, mission accomplished?" he replied.

Rodeo

"My favorite sex position is the rodeo," said Ted.
"What's the rodeo?" asked Fred.
"You get your wife down on her knees and start doing it doggy style, then whisper 'this is your sister's favorite position,' in her ear and try to hold on for 8 seconds!"

Golf Weather

A man pulled out of his garage and was about to go play his usual 18 holes of golf when suddenly a horrible thunderstorm started. He went back in the house, crawled into bed, cuddled up to his still-sleeping wife and whispered in her ear, "The weather's terrible out there. It's a nice day to be in bed."
"Can you believe my jackass husband is out golfing in that crap?" she mumbled.

Flowers

A gloomy looking man walked into a flower shop. He looked so pitiful that the clerk was expecting to sell him funeral flowers. He was quite surprised when the man asked that anniversary flowers be sent to his wife.
"And what day will that be, sir?" the clerk asked.
"Yesterday," the man sighed.

Hypothetically

A boy was doing his homework asked his father, "What's the difference between hypothetical and reality?"
"Go ask your mother if she'd sleep with the mailman for $500,000," his father replied.
The boy went upstairs then returned a few moments later and said, "Yes, she'd sleep with the mailman for $500,000."
"Okay," his father replied, now go ask your sister if she'd sleep with her principal for $500,000."
The boy went upstairs again, then returned a few moments later and said, "She said yes, too."
"Now see how that works?" the father asked. "Hypothetically, we'd be rich. In reality, we're living with two whores."

Bless Me Father

An old man went to confessions and said to the priest, "Father, I'm a 90 year old married man, but last night I had an orgy with two 18 year old girls and made love to each of them twice."
"I see," said the priest. "When was the last time you were in confessions?"
"Never," the man replied. "I'm Jewish."
"Then why are you telling me?" the priest asked.
"I'm telling everyone," the man replied.

Holy Typo

A new monk at a monastery was assigned to help the other monks in hand copying the old writings. He noticed that they were copying from previous copies though, not from the original books, so he went to the head monk to ask him about it. He pointed out that since they were copying from copies, if an error was ever made, it would be continued in all future copies.

"We've been copying from copies for centuries, my son, but you make a valid point," the head monk replied. "I shall go to the cellar and compare our copies to the original books."

Several hours later, noise was heard coming from the cellar and the other monks went to investigate. They found the head monk weeping loudly over one of the original books.

"What is wrong?" they asked.

"The word is *celebrate*!" he sobbed.

Poison

A man said to his priest, "I have a terrible problem, Father. I have to talk to you."

"What's wrong, my son?" the priest asked.

"My wife is trying to poison me," the man replied.

"Why do you say that?" the priest asked.

"Because it's true," the man replied. "What should I do?"

"I can't believe that could be true. Let me talk to her and see what I can find out," the priest said.

A few days later, the priest called the man and said, "I spoke with your wife today. We talked on the phone for over two hours. Do you want my advice?"

"Yes," the man answered eagerly.

"Take the poison," the priest sighed.

Cannibal Cookin

Two cannibals were talking and the first said, "I just can't seem to get a tender missionary. I've baked them, I've roasted them, I've stewed them. I just can't seem to make them tender."

"What kind of missionaries are you using?" the second asked.

"You know, the ones with those brown hooded cloaks with the really baggy sleeves," the first replied.

"No wonder," replied the second. "those are friars!"

Who's the Guy

After a long night of lovemaking, a man pulled out a cigarette and asked the woman for a light.

"I think there's a lighter in the top drawer," she replied.

He opened the drawer and found the lighter, and also noticed an 8x10 picture of a man.

"Who's this, your husband?" he asked nervously.

"No, silly," she replied, snuggling up to him.

"Your boyfriend?" he asked.

"No, there's no one else," she said, nibbling on his ear.

"Well, who is he then?" he demanded.

"That's me before my operation," she replied.

Honeymoon

A small tourist hotel was all abuzz about an afternoon wedding of an 85 year old groom to a 22 year old bride. The general sentiment was that the honeymoon might be too much for his heart to take. But the next morning, it was the bride who stumbled down the staircase looking all worn out and frazzled.

"What happened to you, honey?" the clerk asked.

"Oh God!" she exclaimed. "He told me he had been saving up for 40 years, but I thought he meant his money!"

Math Lesson

A mathematics professor sent a fax to his wife which read:
"Dear Wife, You must realize that you are now 54 years old and you are no longer able to satisfy certain needs which I have. I am otherwise basically happy with you as a wife and I hope you will not be hurt to learn that, by the time you read this, I will be at the Hilton Hotel with my 18 year old student. I'll be home before morning. - Your Husband"

Later at the hotel, a letter was delivered to his room:
"Dear Husband, You too are 54 years old and by the time you receive this, I will be at the Sheraton Hotel with the 18 year old neighbor boy. And being the brilliant mathematician that you are, I'm sure you will realize that 18 can go into 54 easier than 54 can go into 18. See you soon. - Your Wife"

Be Strong

A man escaped from prison after 10 years, broke into a nearby house and found a young couple in bed. He ordered the guy out of bed and tied him to a chair. Then he tied the girl to the bed, kissed her neck, then got up and went into the bathroom.

While he was in the bathroom, the husband said to his wife, "This guy's an escaped prisoner, look at his clothes! He probably hasn't seen a woman in years. I saw how he kissed your neck. If he wants sex, don't resist him. Do whatever he says. He's probably very dangerous and if he gets mad, he might kill us. Be strong, honey. I love you."

His wife replied, "He wasn't kissing my neck, he was whispering in my ear. He told me he thought you were cute and asked if we had any vaseline. I told him it was in the bathroom. Be strong, honey. I love you too!"

On the Hill

The sheriff of a small town apprehended a hillbilly walking around town wearing nothing but his boots. "Why the hell are you walking all over town naked like that?" he demanded.

"It's a long story," the hillbilly replied.

"I got plenty of time," the sheriff replied.

"Well, me and this girl, see, we just met up by the stables and was talkin then we just started cuddling and then some kissin until she said that if we was gonna be sparkin, we oughta go up on the hill, so we did, and up on the hill we started kissing and cuddling some more and then she took off her clothes and she said that I should too, and so I took off all my clothes except fer my boots, and then she lay on the ground and opened up her legs, and then for no reason, she tole me to go to town..."

Honeymoon

A bride said to her husband on their honeymoon, "Honey, I've had a very sheltered life and I don't want to disappoint you tonight. Could you teach me about sex?"

"Sure," he replied. "Let's make it easy. We'll call your private place The Prison, and we'll call my thing The Prisoner. All we do is put the prisoner in the prison." He then made love to her.

A moment later, she said, "Honey, the prisoner escaped."

"Then we'll just have to re-imprison him," he replied with a smile, and he made love to her again.

As soon as they were finished, she giggled and said, "Honey, the prisoner escaped again."

He obliged her again, then wearily stretched out on the bed.

"Honey, the prisoner escaped again," she giggled.

"Now look," he yelled, "it was NOT a life sentence, OK?"

Cigarettes

A man told his wife he was going to the store for cigarettes and would be right back. On his way, he stopped at the bar for one quick beer, but instead, had a few too many, met a beautiful young woman and ended up at her apartment in bed. When he sobered up and realized it was 3 a.m., he asked the woman for some talcum powder, then rubbed the powder all over his hands and went home.

When he arrived home, his furious wife was waiting up for him. "Five hours to get cigarettes?" she screamed. "Where the hell were you all night?"

"Well, to tell you the truth," he began, "I went to a bar, had a few beers, went home with a gorgeous babe and slept with her."

"Let me see your hands!" she demanded, as she examined his powdery hands. "Friggin liar, you were at the pool hall!"

Last Request

A husband and wife had four sons. Their three older sons had dark hair and eyes. Their youngest son had light hair, blue eyes and freckles. The husband was on his deathbed and said to his wife, "Before I die, I have to know. Is our youngest my child?"

"I swear on all things holy that he is yours," she answered. She warmly smiled and tenderly squeezed his hand, thinking to herself, "Thank God he didn't ask about the other three."

Three Days

One Friday after work, a married man went out partying and stayed out for the entire weekend. When he finally went home on Sunday evening, his furious wife screamed at him for nearly two hours before concluding with, "And, how would you like it if I didn't come home for three days?"

"That'd be fine with me," he replied.

Well, Monday came and he didn't see her all day. Tuesday and Wednesday, he didn't see her at all either. Finally, on Thursday, the swelling had gone down just enough so that he was able to see her a little with his left eye.

Toreador Special

A man was visiting Mexico and went to see a bullfight. When the event was over, he went into the restaurant next to the arena. While waiting to be seated, he noticed a waiter serving a delicious looking dish at another table and asked him about it.

"That is called the Toreador Special," the waiter explained. "It is chili and testicles. We get them after the bullfight."

"I just have to try that," the man said.

"I'm very sorry, senor," the waiter replied, "but there is only one dinner available each evening."

"I understand," said the man, and he ordered some tacos.

The next evening, he returned to the restaurant with hopes of trying the "Toreador Special," but just as a he was being seated, he saw a waiter bringing it to another customer. "Damn, I missed it again," he thought. "I must get here earlier."

The following evening, he went to the restaurant and got in line earlier. This time, he was the first one seated and proudly said to the waiter, "I'll have the Toreador Special!"

"Very well, senor!" the waiter replied.

A few minutes later, dinner was served.

When the man had finished eating, the waiter came to his table and asked, "How was your meal, senor?"

"It was delicious," the man replied, "but the 'meatballs' seemed to be a lot smaller tonight."

"I am very sorry, senor," the waiter replied, "but you see, the bull does not always lose."

Oh Nuts

Frank was teaching his friend Jim how to hunt. "Stand still and don't make a sound," he instructed. "I'll try to drive some deer back this way." He then went on ahead to look for deer.

After a few minutes, he heard a loud scream, ran back to Jim and asked, "What the hell happened? What was that scream?"

"Well," Jim began, "there was a big snake and it slithered across my feet, but I didn't scream. Then, a huge bear came up to me and snarled, but I still didn't scream. In fact, I was doing really good, until two squirrels crawled up inside my pants and I heard one ask the other if they should eat them now or take them home."

Camel

A new commander had just arrived at an army base in Saudi Arabia. During his first inspection of the base, he noticed a camel tied to a tree and asked what it was for. One of the soldiers explained that when the men get lonely and there are no women on the base, they use the camel.

A few weeks later, the commander was feeling especially lonely and ordered a couple of soldiers to bring the camel to his tent. The soldiers complied.

About an hour later, the commander emerged from his tent with a huge smile. "So, that's what you men do during these lonely times, eh?" he asked one of the soldiers.

"Well no, sir," the soldier replied. "We usually just ride him into town to meet women."

Parrots

A woman approached her priest and said, "I have two talking female parrots, but they only say one thing, and it's not very nice, Father"

"What do they say?" asked the priest.

"Hi, we're prostitutes. Want to have some fun?" she replied.

"That's terrible!" the priest exclaimed. "But I have an idea! Bring them to my house and we'll put them in the cage with my male parrots. I've taught them to pray and say the rosary, so they should be a very good influence on yours."

"That sounds like a wonderful idea, Father!" she replied.

The next day, she brought her females to his house, and just as he had said, his males were in their cage, holding rosary beads and praying.

"I hope this works, Father," she said.

"I'm very confident," he replied.

The woman watched in anticipation as the priest carefully placed her females into the males' cage.

The females weren't even in the cage two seconds when they started saying, "Hi, we're prostitutes, want to have some fun?"

The males looked at the females, then bowed their heads and proclaimed joyously, "Praise the Lord, our prayers have been answered!"

Monkey Fun

A man walked into a bar with his pet monkey and ordered a drink. While he was drinking, the monkey started jumping all over and eating all the peanuts on the bar. Then he jumped on the pool table, stuck the cue ball in his mouth and swallowed it.

"Did you see what your friggin monkey just did?" the bartender screamed.

"No, what?" the man replied.

"He swallowed the cue ball!" the bartender yelled.

"Yeah, that doesn't surprise me, he eats everything. I'll pay for the cue ball and whatever else he ate," the man replied, then finished his drink, paid his bill and left.

A week later, the man and monkey returned. As before, the

monkey was jumping all over and creating a disturbance, but the worst came when he found a maraschino cherry, stuck it in his butt, then pulled it out and ate it.

"Did you see what your rotten little monkey did now?" the bartender asked in disgust.

"No, what?" the man asked.

"He put a cherry up his butt, then pulled it out and ate it!" replied the bartender.

"Yea, that doesn't surprise me," the man replied. "Ever since he swallowed that cue ball, he measures everything first."

Robby Rooster

A farmer who owned several hundred hens, purchased a very expensive $1000 rooster named Robby to service them. The farmer was hesitant at first about spending so much for one rooster, but the breeder assured him that Robby was the best.

When he brought Robby home, he set him down in the barnyard and said, "I want you to pace yourself. You have a lot of hens to service here, and you cost me a lot of money." He then set him loose and Robby took off towards the henhouse. In just 2 hours, Robby had serviced every hen in the henhouse!

The farmer was shocked, but not nearly as shocked as when, just moments later, Robby was in the duck coop servicing all the ducks! After that, Robby went after a flock of geese by the pond. By sunset Robby was out in the fields chasing and servicing quail and pheasants! The farmer was quite worried now that his $1000 rooster wouldn't last another day, and he said a long prayer before going to bed.

But the next morning, there lie Robby in the barnyard with buzzards circling overhead. As the saddened farmer bent down to pick up Robby's lifeless body, he said, "Oh Robby, I told you to pace yourself. I tried to warn you."

Suddenly, Robby slightly opened one eye, motioned toward the buzzards in the sky and said, "Shh, they're getting closer!"

Vampire Bat

A vampire bat, covered in fresh blood, came home to the cave and the other bats demanded to know where he got it.

"Leave me alone!" he demanded.

They nagged and nagged, however, until he finally gave in.

"Just follow me," he sighed, as he flew out of the cave.

The other bats followed close behind, and through the night they soared, over ponds, around mountain peaks and through trees. Finally, the bat slowed down and the other bats eagerly hovered around him.

"Are we here, are we here?" they asked eagerly.

"See that wall over there?" he asked.

"Yes, Yes, Yes!" they squealed with anticipation.

"Good," he said. "I didn't!"

Wittle Wabbit

A little girl marched into the local pet shop and said to the owner, "Excuth me, mither, do you have any wittle wabbits?"

"We sure do young lady, he said. "Would you wike a wittle white wabbit, a fuwwy bwack wabbit or a bwown wabbit?"

The little girl glared at him for a moment, then rolled her eyes and said, "I don't think my pyfon weally gives a thit."

Gorilla Love

An Alabama wild animal park had a female gorilla which had gone into heat and was becoming quite unruly. They had no male gorillas, so they really had a problem.

The park administrators noticed Hank, a big, strong part-time employee at the park. Hank appeared to be built well enough for the task, so they asked him if he'd be willing to have sex with the gorilla for $500. Hank said he'd have to think it over.

The next day, Hank met with the administrators again and said he would accept their offer, but only under three conditions.

"First," he began, "I don't want no one watchin."

"Ok," they agreed. "We'll fix up a nice private spot for you."

"Second, you can never tell anyone," he continued.

"Ok," they agreed.

"Third, I'll need another week to raise the $500."

Lion Taming

Two unemployed men were sitting around talking about their futures, when the first confidently stated that he was going to be a lion tamer.

"A lion tamer?" the second asked in disbelief. "That's crazy, you don't know nothing about lion taming."

"Sure I do," the first replied.

"OK then, tell me this. When that lion comes at you snarling, what are you gonna do?" the second asked.

"Well, I'll take my big wooden chair and jab it at him until he backs down," replied the first.

"Well, what if he knocks it out of the cage?" asked the second.

"Then I'll hit him with my whip," replied the first.

"What if he chews up your whip?" asked the second.

"Then I'll shoot him with my gun," replied the first.

"What if they don't let you carry a gun?" asked the second.

"Then I'll pick up some shit from the cage, throw it in his eyes and make my escape," replied the first.

"What if there ain't no shit in the cage? asked the second.

"If that lion snarls at me, shreds my whip and I don't have no gun," he began, "there WILL BE shit in that cage!"

Paw

A farmboy accidentally overturned his wagon load of corn on a dirt road. A farmer who lived nearby, looked out, saw the boy struggling with the mess and yelled over, "Hey, forget your troubles, come visit a spell. I'll help you with that wagon later."

"That sure is nice of you," the boy answered, "but it's gettin late and I don't think my paw would want me to."

"C'mon, boy," the farmer insisted. "Looks like you could use a rest. We'll get ya on yer way after we eat some vittles."

"Ok," the boy agreed, "but my paw sure ain't gonna like it."

After a delicious dinner, the boy said, "That sure was tasty and I'm much obliged to y'all, but my paw is gonna be real mad."

"Now don't you worry none 'bout that," the farmer said. "I'll sit down with yer paw and explain everything. Where's he at?"

"Under the wagon," replied the boy.

Plane Game

A lawyer on an airplane noticed that the little boy sitting behind him was being a real wiseguy to the stewardesses. The lawyer, thinking he'd have some fun with the boy, turned back to him and said, "Hey kid, wanna play a game?"

"That's stupid," the boy cracked. "Now turn around and don't bother me!"

"But you can win some money," the lawyer persisted.

"Oh yea? the boy asked.

"Yea," replied the lawyer. "Here's how it works. I'll ask you a question and if you don't know the answer, you have to pay me $5. Then, you ask me a question. If I don't know the answer, I have to pay you $5."

"Pfffft, $5 ain't nothin," the boy cracked.

"Ok," the lawyer replied, "how about this? If I can't answer your question, I'll pay you $500!"

"Now yer talkin!" replied the boy.

"I'll start," the lawyer said. "What is the population of San Diego, California?"

The boy didn't know the answer and handed the lawyer $5.

"Thaaaank yooou," the lawyer said smugly, snatchin the money from the boy. "Your turn."

"What has 3 antlers but no ears?" the boy asked.

The lawyer thought and thought, but he was stumped. Finally, he reluctantly counted out $500 and handed it to the boy.

"Thaaank yooou!" the boy replied smugly.

"Well, what's the answer?" demanded the annoyed lawyer.

The boy nonchalantly handed the lawyer $5.

Keep the Motor Running

An 80 year old man married a 22 year old girl and the entire town was abuzz. Nine months later, the woman gave birth to their first child. At the hospital, the nurse came out to congratulate the father. "How do you do it at your age?" she asked.

"Gotta keep the old motor running!" he replied.

The following year, his wife gave birth again and the same nurse said to him, "You're really amazing. How do you do it?"

"Gotta keep the old motor running!" he said with a grin.

The following year, his wife gave birth again, and the same nurse approached him. Before she could say a word, the proud man grinned and said, "Gotta keep the old motor running!"

"Well you better change the oil," the nurse replied. "They're comin out black."

Survival

A rescue team just located a crashed airplane and found the lone survivor chewing on a human bone.

"You can't judge me for this. I had to survive." he said.

"But, your plane just crashed yesterday!" one rescuer yelled.

Nosey Mom

Dave's mother was visiting his apartment for the first time and couldn't help but notice how attractive his roommate Lisa was. She had heard a lot about Lisa, and she suspected a relationship, but seeing her beauty just made her more suspicious. She observed their behavior carefully over the course of the evening and grew more and more suspicious.

Knowing only too well what his mother was thinking, Dave called her aside and said, "Mom, I know what you're thinking, but Lisa and I are just roommates. It's completely innocent."

A few days later, Lisa approached Dave and said, "You know the ceramic porcupine that was on the knick knack shelf? Ever since your mother was here, I can't find it."

"I don't think my mother would've taken it," he replied, "but I'll call her and make sure." With that, he picked up the phone, called his mother and said, "Mom, please forgive me if I'm wrong, but did you happen to take a figurine from here?"

"Son," she began, "please forgive me if I'm wrong, but if your innocent little roommate had been sleeping in her own bed, she would have found that figurine by now."

Cupid at Law

A young man walked into a post office one day and noticed a middle aged man standing at the counter, methodically placing "I Love You" stamps on envelopes adorned with red hearts, then spraying each one with perfume. Curious, he walked over to him and asked, "What are you doing?"

"I'm sending out these Valentines, signed 'Guess who?' to all the married men in my neighborhood," he replied.

"But why?" the young man asked.

"I'm a divorce lawyer," he replied.

Lois

Lois had a heart attack and was rushed to the hospital. While on the operating table, she had a near death experience, saw God and asked him, "Am I dead?"

"No, Lois, you have another 30 years to live," God answered.

After Lois recovered, she figured she'd make the most of those years and went to have liposuction, collagen injections, a face lift, breast implants and a dye job on her hair. A few days after having all this done, she was struck by a bus and killed.

When she got to Heaven, she immediately said to God, "You told me I had another 30 years to live!"

"Lois?" God asked. "I'm sooo sorry! I didn't recognize you!"

Out of Oil

A group of senators and congressmen were addressing elementary school students in the auditorium. The topic was our nation's current oil situation.

"How many of you have heard anything about our country running low on oil?" one of the congressman asked.

Many of the students raised their hands.

"Does anyone know why this may be?" a senator asked.

One little boy yelled, "My Dad says nobody ever checks the oil levels cuz the oil tanks are in Oklahoma, Alaska, and Texas, but all the dipsticks are in Washington!"

Quickie

John and Laura wanted to have a quickie but they lived in a tiny city apartment and their 9 year old son was home. The only way they could think of to get some privacy was to send him out on the balcony and tell him to "report the neighborhood activities." They figured such an "important job" would surely keep him occupied, so out he went. Within moments, he began shouting his "reports" from the balcony:

"The mailman is here!"

"The Andersons are getting company!"

"Three cop cars just whizzed by!"

"The people across the street are making whoopie!"

John and Laura were shocked to hear that come from his mouth! "Why did you say that??" they yelled to him.

"Cuz their kid is out on the balcony too," he answered.

Hey Mom

"Hey mom, how come you're white and Irish but I'm black and Chinese?" a boy asked his mother.

"Don't even ask me that," she sighed. "From what I remember of that party, you're lucky you don't bark."

Young Marriage

Timmy and Cindy were only 10 years old but wanted to get married. Timmy approached Cindy's father and said, "Me and Cindy are in love and I want to ask you for her hand in marriage."

Thinking he'd have some fun with the cute little boy, Cindy's father replied, "Where will you two live?"

"In Cindy's room!" Timmy gleamed. "It's nice, and it's big enough for both of us and all our stuff!"

"But how will you support her?" the father asked.

"I make $40 a week on my paper route!" Timmy piped.

"What if you have little ones of your own?" the father asked.

"Well," Timmy said, "we've been lucky so far."

Don't Cry

A little boy came running downstairs sobbing his eyes out.
"What's the matter now?" his mother asked.
"Daddy was hanging a picture upstairs and he hit his thumb with the hammer," the boy sobbed.
"Aww, that's no big deal," soothed his mother. "I know you're upset, honey, but a big boy like you shouldn't be crying about such things. Why didn't you just laugh?"
"I did," he sobbed.

Definitely Correct

A third grade teacher told her class that the word for the day was 'definitely,' then asked who could use it in a sentence.
"The sky is definitely blue," said one little boy.
"That isn't really correct. Sometimes the sky is gray, black or even red." the teacher replied.
"Grass is definitely green," a little girl answered.
"That's really not correct either," the teacher replied. "Grass is brown sometimes if it doesn't get water."
"Do farts have lumps?" a little boy shouted out.
"No, and that question is inappropriate!" the teacher scolded.
"But, I definitely shit my pants!" the boy replied.

Farm Tale

A farmer and his wife were relaxing in bed when he looked up from the magazine he was reading and said, "Did you know that human beings are the only species in which the female has an orgasm?"
She looked at him flirtatiously and said, "Prove it!"
"Okay," he said, and he left the room, leaving his wife with a confused look on her face.

An hour later, he returned and proclaimed, "The cow and the goat didn't, but the way that pig is always squealing, I just couldn't tell."

Fun in the Men's Room

A drunk got up from his bar stool and staggered to the men's room. A few minutes later, a loud scream was heard. Shortly afterwards, another loud scream was heard and the bartender finally went to check on the drunk.
  "What's all the screaming about in there?" he shouted through the door. "You're scaring the customers!"
  "I'm just sitting here," the drunk began, "and every time I try to flush, something comes up and squeezes my testicles."
  Hearing that, the bartender opened the door and looked in."You idiot!" he yelled. "You're sitting on the mop bucket!"

Sex Therapy

A man said to his therapist, "I have a serious psychological problem, Doc. I'm no longer able to get aroused by my wife."
  "I see," said the therapist. "Many things can cause problems like this. I'd like to have you both back here tomorrow."
  When the couple returned the next day, the therapist had the wife remove her clothes and lie on the table. He then walked slowly around the table, carefully examining her. "You're fine," he said to the husband. "She doesn't make *me* horny either."

Dreams

"I dreamt that I was at a penis auction," a wife said to her husband. "The long ones were going for a hundred dollars, and the thick ones were going for a hundred and fifty dollars."

"How about ones like mine?" he asked.
"Those were being given away as party favors!" she replied.
"Well, I dreamt that I was at a vagina auction," he said. "The pretty ones were going for seven hundred dollars, and the cute little tight ones were going for for nine hundred."
"What about ones like mine?" she asked.
"That's where they held the auction!" he quipped.

Trade

My girlfriend and I were doing a photo shoot on a ranch in Texas when the owner of the neighboring ranch called us over.
"She your woman?" he asked.
"Yea," I replied.
"From the size of them breasts, I figure she's gotta be a good ole Texas gal! Am I right?" he asked.
"Nope, we're both from PA," I answered.
"Dang," he said. "Well anyhow, she's reeal purdy. I'll give ya 20 head of Angus cattle for her."
After a few seconds, my girlfriend elbowed me, prompting me to answer, "Naa, she's not for sale."
As we got back to our work, she asked me, "What took you so long to answer that creep?"
"I was trying to figure how to get 20 cows home," I replied.

Star Tiff

Dr. McCoy walked onto the bridge, limping, bruised and looking all beat up.
"Bones, what happened?" Captain Kirk asked.
"I got in a tiff with private Conners," McCoy answered.
"Conners? Isn't he that little guy from engineering?" Kirk asked. "He must have had something in his hand to hurt you like that."

"Aye, that he did, " McCoy replied. "A shovel it was."

"Didn't you have anything in your hand?" Kirk asked.

"Aye Captain, that I did, Mrs. Conners' left tit, and a beautiful thing it was. . but not very much good in a fight."

Memories

An old man was strolling through his hometown taking in the landmarks and reflecting back on his life.

"I remember helping to build the bridges in this town when I was 24. I worked hard for many months. But people don't call you 'the bridge builder' if you do that. No, they don't."

"I remember helping to build the school when I was 30. But people don't call you 'the school builder' for doing that. No, not in this town."

"I remember building all the pavilions in the park when I was 35. But people don't call you 'the pavilion builder' for doin that, no, they don't."

"But screw just one goat..."

Handout

College students Jim and Paul were standing on a corner in New York City when a beggar approached them and asked for some spare change. Jim rejected the beggar in disgust, but Paul quickly pulled a couple of bills from his wallet and handed them to him. The beggar thanked him and walked away.

Jim was furious and scolded, "Why did you give him that? He's only gonna use it to buy drugs or booze!"

"What, and we weren't?" Paul replied.

Don't We Look Pretty

An elderly woman was at the gynecologist's office for a routine exam. As the doctor placed the woman's legs in the stirrups and was about to begin the exam, he remarked, "My, don't we look pretty today!"

The woman was shocked, but didn't say a word.

That evening, the woman was telling her 30 year old daughter about the incident and asked, "Wasn't that a highly inappropriate thing for him to say?"

"I don't know," her daughter replied. "Maybe he was just referring to your perm or your new eyeglasses."

"No," the woman replied. "He was looking *down there* when he said it."

"Maybe it was your perfume," said the daughter. "Maybe he said you *smelled* pretty. After all, your hearing has been giving you trouble lately."

"I didn't wear perfume today," the woman replied. "Come to think of it though, I did spray some of your feminine spray down there this morning."

"I don't have any feminine spray," the daughter said.

"Sure you do," replied the woman. "The tall pink can on the bathroom sink."

"Mom," the daughter replied, "that's your grandaughter's sparkle hair glitter."

Who's Cheating

A woman just hung up from a brief telephone call.

"Who was that?" her date asked.

"My husband," she replied.

"I better get going," he said nervously.

"Relax, he won't be home for hours," she replied. "He's at the pool hall with you."

Sibling Prom

Hank and his sister Marilou couldn't find no dates to take 'em to the prom, so Hank was fixin to stay home.

"We oughta go the prom together!" Marilou said.

"No, you're my sister. It won't be no fun," Hank replied.

"Come on!" Marilou persisted. "It'll be plenty fun!"

Hank finally agreed and they went to the prom together. When they arrived, she asked him to dance.

"No, you're my sister. It won't be no fun," Hank replied.

"Come on, it'll be plenty fun," Marilou goaded.

So, they danced several dances and had a good time. When the prom was over, Marilou asked Hank to take her to makeout hill.

"No, you're my sister. It won't be no fun," he replied.

"We'll just talk," she replied. "We don't never talk no more."

So, they drove to makeout hill, but instead of talkin, Marilou climbed into the backseat and said, "Take me, Hank!"

With no argument, Hank climbed back and got on top of her.

"You're lots lighter than Paw," she said.

"Yea," he replied. "Maw told me that just the other night."

Bang

An 85 year old man was having his annual checkup and the doctor asked him how he was feeling.

"I'm feeling great, Doc!" he boasted. "I have a sexy 19 year old bride who's pregnant with my baby!

"That's great!" the doctor said. "I knew a guy once who was a big-time hunter. He spotted a huge grizzly bear one afternoon, then realized he had left his rifle in the truck. The bear had him cornered, so he picked up a branch from the ground, pointed it at the bear, and BANG. . Shot the bear dead!"

"That impossible!" the old man exclaimed. "I don't believe a word of it. Someone else must have shot the bear."

"That was sort of my point," replied the doctor.

Playing Doctor

A mother discovered her young daughter and the neighbor's boy playing doctor in the bedroom. The furious mother grabbed the telephone and called the boy's mother.

"I just caught your rotten kid playing doctor with my daughter!" yelled the mother.

"Calm down," the boy's mother replied. "It's normal for children of their age to play doctor and explore their sexuality."

"Sexuality?? He removed her friggin appendix!" the mother bellowed.

Dopey Meets The Pope

The Seven Dwarfs were ushered in to meet the Pope and were now standing just 25 feet away from his podium.

"Does anyone have any questions for me?" the Pope asked.

"Dopey wants to ask you a question!" Sneezy said.

"No I don't!" Dopey snapped.

"Yes he does," Sneezy persisted. "Now ask him, Dopey."

"You can ask me," said the Pope. "Don't be shy."

"Yea, Dopey, don't be shy," Sneezy goaded. "Ask him!"

"Um, are there nuns in Alaska?" Dopey finally asked.

"Yes, of course," the Pope answered.

"Ok, thank you," Dopey said.

"No, no, no!" the other dwarfs teased. "You're not done yet, Dopey! Finish asking him."

"Shut up, you guys!" Dopey scolded under his breath.

"Do you have another question, Dopey?" the Pope asked.

"Yes, he does, Your Majesty!" Sneezy interjected, as he gave Dopey a solid shove forward.

Now trapped alone and way out in front of the group, Dopey nervously asked, "Um, are there any black nuns in Alaska?"

"Yes, Dopey, I'm sure there are," the Pope replied. "The convent is open to all races."

"Ok, thank you," Dopey said, and retreated back to the group.

"Unt uh, Dopey!" the other dwarfs teased again. "You're not done yet! Finish the question!"

"Shut up, you guys!" Dopey scolded under his breath.

"Dopey wants to ask you another question," Sneezy chimed.

Dopey elbowed him and said, "Shut UP! No I DON'T!"

"*Do* you have another question, Dopey?" the Pope asked.

"Yes, he DOES!" Sneezy interjected as he again shoved Dopey towards the Pope.

"And what is your question, Dopey?" the Pope asked.

Dopey, way out in front of the group again, fidgeted and looked at the floor, then looked back at the other dwarfs, then looked at the floor again and finally asked in a meek little voice, "Are there any black nuns in Alaska that are midgets?"

"No, there aren't, Dopey," the Pope answered.

The other dwarfs burst into laughter and chanted, "Dopey screwed a penguin, Dopey screwed a penguin. . ."

Disgrace

A blonde was about to go on her first date and her grandmother sat her down for a talk..

"The boy might try to kiss you," she said. "He might also try to touch your breasts or put his hand in your pants, so be careful. Most importantly though, if he tries to get on top of you and have his way with you, DO NOT let him. That would disgrace our family."

The next day the blonde told her grandmother, "It was just like you said! He kissed me, touched my breasts and put his hand in my pants! But when he tried to disgrace our family, I fixed him good! I got on top of him and disgraced his family!"

Fishy Story

A man phoned his wife from work and told her that a big client had insisted that he accompany him on a weekend fishing trip. Explaining that he had to leave soon, he asked her to pack his fishing gear, three days of clothes, and his favorite robe. An hour later, he picked up the stuff, kissed her goodbye and left.

When he returned after the trip, his wife asked how it was.

"The fishing was great!" he replied. "The cabin was nice, but it was a bit chilly, and you forgot to pack my robe."

"No I didn't," she replied. "It was in your tackle box."

Zoomin Granny

An old lady was zooming up and down the halls of the nursing home and making car noises in her wheelchair. Suddenly, an old man grabbed the back of her wheelchair and brought her to a stop. "I pulled you over because you were speeding," he said. Can I see your driver's license?"

The old lady pulled out a candy wrapper from her nightgown pocket and handed it to him. He looked it over and let her go with just a warning.

Half an hour later, she was still zooming around the facility until the man stopped her again. "Now, you were driving recklessly," he said. "I'll need to see your registration."

She pulled an old raffle ticket from her purse and handed it to him. He examined it and let her go with a warning.

Half an hour later, she was still zooming around the facility, making even more noise than before, until the old man stopped her again. "I think you've been drinking," he said. This time, however, he steered her to his room and pulled down his pants.

"Uh oh," she said, "it's the breathalyzer!"

Shirt Tale

Fred was getting dressed for a night out with his friends.

"You're not going out!" yelled his wife. All you ever do is get drunk and puke on your clothes!"

"I promise not to drink tonight, honey," he begged.

He was finally allowed to go out, but sure enough, two hours later, he was drunk and had already puked on his shirt.

"My wife is gonna kill me," he said to his friend. "I puked all over my shirt, after promising her I wouldn't drink tonight."

"No problem," his friend replied. "Go home with a $10 bill in your hand, then, tell your wife that some drunk puked on your shirt and gave you the money to pay for cleaning."

When Fred got home that night, his wife saw the puke on his shirt. "I knew you'd get drunk and puke on your shirt!" she screamed.

"I wasn't drinking," he said. "Some drunk guy puked on my shirt. He even gave me this $10 to pay for cleaning!"

She grabbed the money from this hand, but there were two $10 bills. "Then what's the other $10 bill for?" she demanded.

"That's from the guy who pissed on my pants," he said.

One Night on a Train

A man and a woman who had never met, found themselves in the same sleeping car of a train. Despite their embarrassment, they agreed to make the best of the situation and go to sleep. The man took the top bunk and the woman took the lower. In the middle of the night, the man reached down, woke the woman and said, "I'm sorry to wake you, but I'm really cold. Could you get me another blanket?"

"I have a better idea," the woman said wistfully. "Just for tonight, let's pretend that we're married!"

"Ok, great!" the man replied, as he eagerly climbed down.

"Good," the woman replied. "get your own blanket."

Blonde Shorts

Q. Did you hear about the new blonde paint?
A. It's not real bright, but its cheap and it spreads easy.

Q. What did the blonde's right leg say to the left leg?
A. Nothing. They haven't met.

Q. What's a blonde's favorite nursery rhyme?
A. Humpme Dumpme.

Q. Why don't blondes use vibrators?
A. They chip their teeth.

Q. How can you tell a blonde has had a bad day?
A. She has a tampon tucked behind her ear and she can't find her pencil.

Q. How did the blonde burn her nose?
A. Bobbing for french fries.

Q. What do you call a blonde with 2 brain cells?
A. Pregnant.

Q. What's the difference between a blonde and a 747?
A. Not everyone has been in a 747.

Q. What should you do if a blonde throws a grenade at you?
A. Pull the pin and throw it back.

Q. What do blondes and cow shit have in common?
A. The older they get, the easier they are to pick up.

Q. How does a blonde turn on the light after sex?
A. She opens the car door.

Q. What do smart blondes and UFOs have in common?
A. You sometimes hear about them, but rarely see one.

Q. Why did the blonde stare at the can of frozen orange juice?
A. The label said concentrate.

Q. What's the difference between a blonde and the Titanic?
A. They know how many went down on the Titanic.

Q. Why do blondes wear underwear?
A. To keep their ankles warm.

Q. What's the difference between a blonde and a brick?
A. The brick doesn't follow you home after you lay it.

Q. Why did the blonde sell her car?
A. She needed gas money.

Q. What do you call a blonde in the closet?
A. The 2008 hide-and-seek champion.

Q. How can you tell when a fax is from a blonde?
A. It has a stamp on it.

Q. How do you drown a blonde?
A. Put a mirror at the bottom of the pool.

Q. What did the blonde say when she saw the banana peel?
A. Uh oh, I'm gonna fall again!

Q. How can you tell when a blonde has used your computer?
A. There's White Out on the screen.

Q. What's the difference between sunglasses and a blonde?
A. Sunglasses sit higher on your face.

Q. Why do blondes always drink with straws?
A. Practice.

Q. What did the blonde's left leg say to her right leg?
A. Between both of us, we can make a lot of money.

Q. Why do blondes put their hair in ponytails?
A. To cover the valve.

Q. Why should blondes not be given coffee breaks?
A. It takes too long to retrain them.

Q. What's the difference between a blonde and a male?
A. The blonde has a higher sperm count.

Q. What's the difference between a group of blondes and a good magician?
A. The magician has a cunning array of stunts.

Q. What do blondes say after making love?
A. Are you boys all on the same team?

Q. What do blondes and turtles have in common?
A. Once on their back, they're screwed.

Q. Why did the blonde have T.G.I.F. written on her sneakers?
A. Toes Go In First.

Q. How do you make a blonde laugh on Monday morning?
A. Tell her a joke on Friday afternoon.

Q. Why do blondes have so much free time?
A. Because so little is expected of them.

Q. How many blondes does it take to screw in a light bulb?
A. They only screw in cars.

Q. What's the first thing a blonde does in the morning?
A. Goes home.

Q. Why did God give blondes one more brain cell than horses?
A. So when they're waving in a parade, they won't crap in the street.

Q. If Tarzan and Jane were blondes, what would Cheetah be?
A. The smartest of the three.

Q. Why did it take the blonde a year to drive to CA from NY?
A. Because of all the "Clean Restrooms Ahead" signs.

Q. Why don't blondes make good pharmacists?
A. They can't get the little bottle in the typewriter.

Q. Why did the blonde get fired from the M&M factory?
A. She kept throwing away all the Ws.

Q. What did the blonde say when she learned she was pregnant?
A. Is it mine?

Q. Why did the blonde wear condoms on her ears?
A. So she wouldn't get hearing aids.

Q. What's the difference between a smart blonde and bigfoot?
A. Bigfoot has been sighted.

Q. Why didn't the blonde like duck hunting?
A. She couldn't throw her dog high enough.

Q. Why did the blonde drive around the block all day?
A. Her turn signal was stuck.

Q. What do you call twelve blondes sitting in a circle.
A. A dope ring.

Q. How do blondes get holes in their forehead?
A. Learning to eat with a fork.

Q. How do you measure a blonde's I.Q.
A. With a tire gauge.

Q. Why was the blonde mad at the Driver's License Bureau?
A. Because they gave her an "F" in sex.

Q. Why can't blondes dial 911?
A. They can't find the eleven on the phone.

Q. How do you get a blonde on the roof?
A. Tell her the drinks are on the house.

Q. Why did the blonde call the welfare office?
A. She wanted to know how to cook her food stamps.

Q. What did the blonde say at the YMCA?
A. They spelled Macy's wrong.

Q. What did the blonde say when she looked in the box of Cheerios?
A. Cool, donut seeds!

Q. Why are some blondes' breasts square?
A. They forget to take the tissue out of the box.

Q. Why do blondes wear their bangs curled up?
A. So things don't go over their heads.

Q. Which 3rd grader should you date, a brunette or a blonde?
A. The blonde. She's 21.

Chauvinist Shorts

Q. How many men does it take to open a beer?
A. It should be open by the time she brings it.

Q. Why is a laundromat a really bad place to pick up a woman?
A. Because a woman who can't afford a washing machine won't make a good provider.

Q. Why do women have smaller feet than men?
A. So they can stand closer to the sink.

Q. How do you know when a woman's about to say something smart?
A. She starts her sentence with "A man once told me..."

Q. What kind of watch should you buy your wife?
A. None. There's a perfectly good clock on the stove.

Q. Why do men pass gas more than women?
A. Women don't shut up long enough to build up pressure.

Q. Why were shopping carts invented?
A. To teach women to walk on their hind legs.

Q. What's worse than a male chauvinist?
A. A woman who doesn't do what she's told.

Q. What do you say to a woman with two black eyes?
A. Nothing. You already told her twice.

Q. Why do women wear white on their wedding day?
A. The dishwasher is supposed to match the other appliances.

Miscellaneous Shorts

Q. What does it mean when the doctor says you have six months to live?
A. You have five months to pay.

Q. When does a doctor suggest emergency surgery?
A. When he's ready for a new sports car.

Q. How can you tell if you have a cheap doctor?
A. He takes Friday off to play miniature golf.

Q. What's the difference between light and hard?
A. You can sleep with a light on.

Q. Why do women rub their eyes when they get out of bed?
A. Because they don't have balls to scratch.

Q. Why is sex like a bridge game?
A. You don't need a partner if you have a good hand.

Q. What's the definition of mixed emotions?
A. Your mother-in-law backing off a cliff in your new car.

Q. What's the height of conceit?
A. Having an orgasm and yelling your own name.

Q. What's the definition of macho?
A. Jogging home from your own vasectomy.

Q. What does a Christmas tree and a priest have in common?
A. Their balls are just for decoration.

Q. Why don't blind people like to sky dive?
A. Because it scares the hell out of the dog.

Q. What does the LAPD and the Green Bay Packers have in common?
A. Neither can stop a Bronco.

Q. What's the difference between a lawyer and God?
A. God doesn't think he's a lawyer.

Q. Why is divorce so expensive?
A. Because it's worth it.

Q. Did you hear about the dyslexic devil worshipper?
A. He sold his soul to Santa.

Q. How do crazy people go through the woods?
A. They take the psycho path.

Q. How do you get holy water?
A. Boil the hell out of it.

Q. How does a spoiled rich girl change a light bulb?
A. She says, "Daddy, I want a new apartment."

Q. What did the fish say when he hit a concrete wall?
A. Dam.

Q. What do Eskimos get from sitting on the ice too long?
A. Polaroids.

Q. What do prisoners use to call each other?
A. Cell phones.

Q. What does D.N.A. stand for?
A. National Dyslexics Association.

Q. What do you call a boomerang that doesn't work?
A. A stick.

Q. What do you call cheese that isn't yours?
A. Nacho Cheese.

Q. What do you call Santa's helpers?
A. Subordinate Clauses.

Q. What do you call four bull fighters in quicksand?
A. Quatro sinko.

Q. What is a zebra?
A. 25 sizes larger than an A bra.

Q. What kind of coffee was served on the Titanic?
A. Sanka.

Q. What lies at the bottom of the ocean and twitches?
A. A nervous wreck.

Q. What's the difference between an oral thermometer and a rectal thermometer?
A. The taste.

Q. Where do you find a no legged dog?
A. Right where you left him.

Q. Where do you get virgin wool?
A. Ugly sheep.

Q. Why are there so many Smiths in the phone book?
A. They all have phones.

Q. Why do bagpipers walk when they play?
A. They're trying to get away from the noise.

Q. Why do gorillas have big nostrils?
A. Because they have big fingers.

Q. How many perverts does it take to put in a light bulb?
A. One, but it takes the entire emergency room to get it out.

Q. Did you hear about the male prostitute who got leprosy?
A. He did good until his business fell off.

Q. How do you piss off Winnie the Pooh?
A. Stick your finger in his honey.

Q. Why are cowgirls bowlegged?
A. Cowboys like to eat with their hats on.

Q. What's the definition of a teenager?
A. God's punishment for enjoying sex.

Q. How is a woman like a road?
A. Both have manholes.

Q. What do you call a truckload of vibrators?
A. Toys for Twats.

Q. What do you call kinky sex with chocolate?
A. S&M&M.

Q. Why do we have orgasms?
A. So we know when to stop.

Q. What's the definition of a transvestite?
A. A guy who likes to eat, drink and be Mary.

Q. Mom's have Mother's Day and Father's have Father's Day. What do single guys have?
A. Palm Sunday.

Q. Why don't debutantes go to orgies?
A. Too many thank you notes to write.

Q. How can you get VD from a toilet seat?
A. By sitting down before the last guy gets up.

Q. What do you call kids born in whorehouses?
A. Brothel sprouts.

Q. What is every Amish woman's private fantasy?
A. Two Mennonite.

Q. What has little balls and screws old ladies?
A. A bingo machine.

Q. What do women and condoms have in common?
A. Both spend more time in your wallet than on your pecker.

Q. How do you make 5 pounds of fat look good?
A. Put a nipple on it.

Q. If Eve wore a fig leaf, what did Adam wear?
A. A hole in it.

Q. How do you spot a blind man in a nudist colony?
A. It's not hard.

Q. Did you hear about the flasher who was thinking of retiring?
A. He decided to stick it out for one more year.

Q. What is a Yankee?
A. The same as a quickie, except no woman is needed.

Q. What does a gynecologist and a pizza delivery boy have in common?
A. They can both smell it, but they can't eat it.

Q. Why don't cannibals eat clowns?
A. They taste funny.

Q. Why doesn't Mexico have an Olympic team?
A. Because everyone who can run, jump, or swim is in the U.S.

Q. What's the definition of a male chauvinist pig?
A. A man who hates every bone in a woman's body except his own.

Q. What's the difference between a pick pocket and a peeping Tom?
A. A pick pocket snatches watches.

Q. Why do the men in Scotland wear kilts?
A. Because the sheep can hear a zipper a mile away.

Q. What is the biggest problem for an atheist?
A. No one to talk to during orgasm.

Q. How do you turn a fox into an elephant?
A. Marry it.

Q. How can you tell if a woman is too fat to have sex with?
A. When you pull her pants down, her ass is still in them.

Q. What is the difference between a drug dealer and a hooker?
A. A drug dealer sells new crack.

Q. How can you tell a macho women?
A. She rolls her own tampons.

Q. Why don't cows laugh?
A. It makes milk come out of their nose.

Q. What are three dreaded words to hear while making love?
A. Honey, I'm home.

Q. Why do women fake orgasm?
A. Because men fake foreplay.

Q. What's the difference between a g-spot and a golfball?
A. A guy will search for a golfball.

Q. What did the elephant say to the naked man?
A. It's cute but can you pick up peanuts with it?

Q. What has four legs and an arm?
A. A happy pit bull.

Fun Things to Say to Pregnant Woman

1. Geez, you're awfully puffy looking today.
2. Are your ankles *supposed* to look like that?
3. The kid must be 50 pounds!
4. I hope your thighs aren't gonna stay flabby.
5. Can they induce labor before the world series starts?
6. Can we name it 'Lola,' after my new secretary?
7. The tattoo on your stomach got huge!
8. I ate all your cookies.
9. And you're *sure* it's not triplets?
10. Looks like it already has a crib.
11. I'm glad us fathers don't get like that.
12. Can you imagine if that was all helium?
13. Quit hoggin the bed, Moby.
14. Oooh a beach ball! Let's play!

– the end –

CPSIA information can be obtained
at www.ICGtesting.com
Printed in the USA
BVHW041831270621
610598BV00013B/571